the lebanese cookbook hussien dekmak

D0351763

the lebanese cookbook

hussien dekmak

with photography by martin brigdale

kyle books

I dedicate this book to the memory of my head chef at Al Hamra, Hassan Mardini, who worked very hard to make me start this journey of cooking special Lebanese food.

This edition reprinted in 2011 by
Kyle Books
23 Howland Street
London W1T 4AY
general.enquiries@kylebooks.com
www.kylebooks.com

First published in Great Britain in 2006 by Kyle Cathie Limited

ISBN 978 1 85626 764 9

Text © 2006 Hussien Dekmak
Photography © 2006 Martin Brigdale
(see also photo credits on page 160)
Book design © 2006 Kyle Books

All rights reserved. No reproduction, copy or transmission of
this publication may be made without written permission. No
paragraph of this publication may be reproduced, copied or
transmitted save with the written permission or in accordance
with the provision of the Copyright Act 1956 (as amended). Any
person who does any unauthorised act in relation to this
publication may be liable to criminal prosecution and civil
claims for damages.

Project editor: Jennifer Wheatley
Designer: Geoff Hayes
Photographer: Martin Brigdale
Food styling: Hussien Dekmak (apart from pages 2, 63 and 75;
            Lucy McElvey)
Styling: Helen Trent
Copy editor: Vanessa Kendell
Editorial assistant: Vicki Murrell
Production: Sha Huxtable & Alice Holloway

Hussien Dekmak is hereby identified as the author of this work
in accordance with Section 77 of the Copyright, Designs and
Patents Act 1988.

A Cataloguing In Publication record for this title is available
from the British Library.

Colour reproduction by Scanhouse
Printed in China by C&C Offset Printing Co., Ltd

contents

Welcome to Lebanon

A beautiful country stretching across a small section of the Mediterranean sea, the Lebanon is famous for its natural landscape, which combines bewitching beaches, glorious mountains and emerald-green fields. *Ahlan-wasahlan* – welcome!

The temperate climate and wonderfully hospitable nature of Lebanon have produced a multitude of delicious recipes that are a pleasure to the eye and a comfort to the heart, so much so that you will want to sample each and every dish, especially the famous Lebanese mezze which is known for its unique flavours. Healthy too, with emphasis on fresh ingredients and aromatic spices, Lebanese food reflects the Mediterranean diet, with an abundance of fresh vegetables, olive oil, garlic, fish, lamb, chicken and grains.

Connoisseurs of Lebanese cuisine will tell you that is that it has exceptional qualities of both taste and variety. *Tabbouleh* (parsley salad); *manakeish bil zahtar* (flatbread baked with thyme, sumac and sesame seeds); *moutabal* (smoky aubergine dip); *ardishawki bil lahma* (artichoke hearts with lamb); *shish taouk* (grilled chicken) – we've put all these and more in this book, so now you can prepare delicious, authentic meals in your own home.

How to put a Lebanese meal together

In Lebanon the table is always full. Soups, salads, mezze and main dishes are all served at the same time and shared around, and there is always bread on the table.

The recipes in this book are traditional, home-style cooking. Most are very straightforward and you'll find you don't need many unusual ingredients. The serving sizes of dishes take into account the fact that they will be presented alongside many others, so most of the starters, or mezze, serve four as part of a larger meal. All Lebanese food is simple and not too heavy, and it's important that the ingredients are as fresh as possible to get the best results (every dish is prepared fresh to order in my restaurant.)

You can entertain for all tastes and appetites by serving a selection of dishes from the various chapters. Although the main courses are all based around meat and fish, the other chapters provide a myriad of options for vegetarians and meat eaters alike with wonderful salads, vegetable and lentil dishes, breads, dips and pastries.

shorbet adas
lentil soup

My daughter's favourite.

Serves 6

200g split red lentils, rinsed
50g butter
1 medium onion, chopped
salt
1 tablespoon ground cumin, plus extra for garnish
lemon wedges, to serve

Place the lentils in a pan, cover with water and bring to the boil. Reduce the heat and cook, covered, for about 30 minutes, topping up with water if necessary.

Heat the butter in a frying pan, add the onion and stir until golden. Add the onion to the lentils along with salt and the cumin. Cook for a further 10 minutes, stirring.

Transfer the lentil mixture to a food-processor and whizz for a few minutes until smooth.

Divide the soup between serving bowls and sprinkle with ground cumin if liked. Serve with lemon wedges and toasted bread.

adas bil hamed
lentil soup with swiss
chard and lemon

ربة سلق وعدس

Serves 4

500g Swiss chard, roughly chopped
100g green or brown lentils, rinsed
1 potato, cut into small cubes
salt and black pepper
1 tablespoon olive oil
2 tablespoons chopped onions
lemon juice

Place the Swiss chard in a pan. Add the lentils and enough water to cover, then bring to the boil and simmer for 15 minutes. Add the potato, salt and pepper and continue to cook until the lentils are cooked. Heat the olive oil in a frying pan and fry the chopped onions until softened.

Add the onions to the lentils and Swiss chard, then pour in lemon juice to taste. Toss together and serve.

If you want to add meat, fry small pieces of lamb (about 100g in total) with the onion at the beginning.

Serves 4

2 tablespoons butter
1/2 onion
2 courgettes, cut into cubes
2 carrots, cut into cubes
1 potato, cut into cubes
1 red pepper, diced
1 green pepper, diced
salt and black pepper
1 teaspoon tomato purée

Heat the butter in a pan, add the onion and stir until softened. Add all the other vegetables and stir until tender. Pour in enough water to cover, and season with salt and black pepper. Bring to the boil, then reduce the heat and add the tomato purée.

Stir and simmer over a medium heat for a further 30 minutes. Serve hot.

shorbet dajaj bil sha'rieh
chicken soup with vermicelli

Serves 4

250g chicken breast, meat on the bone
1 teaspoon butter
1/4 onion, chopped
salt and black pepper
50g vermicelli
1 tablespoon chopped flat parsley

Place the chicken in a large saucepan and cover with 1.5 litres of cold water. Bring to the boil and cook for about 45 minutes or until cooked. Remove the chicken from the pan and reserve the chicken stock.

Tear the chicken into pieces with your hands.

Heat the butter in a saucepan, add the onion and fry until tender. Add the reserved chicken stock with a little salt and pepper and bring to the boil. Simmer for 10 minutes, then reduce the heat and add the chicken and vermicelli. Cook for a further 10–15 minutes or until the vermicelli is soft.

Pour the soup into bowls and garnish with parsley.

As a young boy my family lived in a village called Bayesour in the mountains of Lebanon. My mother used to take me with her to the valley to collect special tea herbs called *zoofa* and *zaizafoon*. She mixed those with other herbs like the ones you see in the picture – dried rose petals, corn husks and bay leaves. These herbal teas or *zhoorat* are mostly drunk in the winter, to protect people from catching colds and to keep them warm. They are also sometimes drunk instead of normal tea.

شوربة الدجاج بالكريم

cream of chicken soup
shorbet al dajaj bil crema

This is very popular with children. The chicken pieces sink to the bottom of the bowl, which makes for a nice surprise.

Serves 6

1 tablespoon butter
1/2 onion, chopped
200g chicken breast, chopped into small chunks
750ml chicken stock
salt and black pepper
200ml double cream
2 tablespoons plain flour

Heat the butter in a saucepan, add the onion and cook, stirring, until browned. Add the chicken and fry, stirring occasionally, until tender.

Pour the chicken stock into the pan and season with salt and pepper. Bring to the boil and cook over a medium heat for 15 minutes. Reduce the heat and stir in the double cream.

Combine the plain flour with 2 tablespoons of water and add to the pan. Cook over a low heat for a further 15 minutes, stirring constantly, so you have a smooth consistency.

Divide the soup between six bowls, season with black pepper and serve.

سلطة الروكا

This salad is especially good with grilled meat dishes (see barbecue recipes on pages 128–130).

Serves 4

2 large handfuls of rocket, roughly chopped
2 tablespoons finely chopped onion
100g radishes, thinly sliced
1 large tomato, finely chopped
1 tablespoon olive oil
juice of $1/2$ lemon
salt

Place the rocket in a bowl and add the onion, radishes and tomato. Add the olive oil, lemon juice and salt and mix well before serving.

salatit batata
potato salad

On hot days this salad makes a light lunch by itself and will serve two instead of four people.

Serves 4

2 large potatoes, boiled
2 spring onions, chopped
1 medium tomato, chopped
1 green pepper, chopped
1 red pepper, chopped
1 tablespoon chopped flat parsley
1 teaspoon chopped mint
$1/2$ tablespoon lemon juice
1 tablespoon olive oil
salt

Cut the potatoes into large cubes and place in a bowl. Add the remainder of the vegetables, the herbs, lemon juice, olive oil and salt. Mix well.

Serve as an appetiser.

Serves 4

50g Kalamata or other black olives, stoned and sliced lengthways
50g green olives, stoned and sliced lengthways
2 tablespoons chopped spring onion
1 medium tomato, chopped
1 tablespoon chopped mint
1 red pepper, chopped
1 tablespoon olive oil
1/2 tablespoon lemon juice
salt

Place all the ingredients in a bowl and toss together well.

Serve as an appetiser.

olive trees

Lebanon is one of the Mediterranean countries famous for growing olive trees. My brother and I used to pick olives from the trees, smash them and eat them with a little bit of salt – it's very tasty but bitter which not everyone likes! Another way to eat them is to dip in *labneh* (see recipe on page 34) and eat as a snack.

Olive trees produce olives every two years. People who live in the mountains and have olive trees on their land harvest them and eat what they can. With the rest, half are stored in jars of oil and half are taken to the olive press in the village (*maasart zaytoon*) to make olive oil to last them until the next harvest.

سلطة مشوية

salatah al khodar al meshweya
grilled vegetable salad

These vegetables can easily be done on a barbecue at the same time as cooking any of the other dishes in the barbecue chapter. If you are doing them this way, you will need to thread the vegetable pieces on to skewers.

Serves 4

2 tomatoes, halved
1 aubergine, cut into large pieces
1 red pepper, cut into large pieces
1 green pepper, cut into large pieces
1 onion, cut into large pieces
1 tablespoon chopped flat parsley
1 tablespoon chopped mint leaves
1 tablespoon olive oil
1 tablespoon lemon juice
salt

Grill the vegetables under a grill or on a barbecue until softened and charred.

Put all the grilled vegetables into a bowl. Add the parsley, mint, olive oil and lemon juice. Add salt to taste and mix together, being careful not to crush the vegetables.

Serve with barbecued meat.

سلطة البندورة والبصل

salatet al banadorah wa al basal
tomato and onion salad

Serves 2

3 tomatoes, roughly chopped
2 tablespoons chopped onions or spring onions
salt
1 teaspoon olive oil
1 tablespoon lemon juice

Place the tomatoes, onions, salt, olive oil and lemon juice in a bowl.

Toss well together and serve with *moujadara* (lentils and rice with crispy onions) (see recipe on page 162).

سلطة الخيار باللبن

salatah khiar bi laban
yogurt with cucumber dip

Serves 4

3 medium cucumbers
250g yogurt (see recipe on page 34) or use shop-bought plain yogurt
1 teaspoon dried mint
2 garlic cloves, crushed
salt

Grate the cucumbers into a bowl. Add the yogurt, mint, garlic and salt and stir to combine.

Serve with *shish taouk* (grilled chicken), *kofta meshwi* (grilled minced lamb on skewers) or with *kibbeh bil sainieh* (baked kibbeh) (see recipes on pages 129, 130 and 82).

salatit malfouf abiad
white cabbage salad

Serves 4

1 small white cabbage
1 tablespoon olive oil
2 tablespoons lemon juice
salt
1 garlic clove, crushed

Chop the cabbage into fine strips, then place in a bowl with the olive oil, lemon juice, salt to taste and garlic. Mix well and serve with *moujadara hamra* (lentils with bulgur wheat) (see recipe on page 195).

salatit zahtar akhdar
fresh thyme salad

Serves 4

100g fresh wild thyme (or use ordinary thyme)
2 tablespoons finely chopped onion
2 tablespoons finely chopped tomatoes
1 tablespoon lemon juice
1 teaspoon olive oil
salt

Remove the thyme leaves from the stems and place in a dish. Add the onion, tomatoes, lemon juice, olive oil and salt to taste. Toss together well.

Serve with grilled meat dishes.

Cos lettuce is the most popular lettuce in Lebanon. This salad is good with barbecued meat.

Serves 4

1 Cos lettuce
1 cucumber
1 medium tomato
small handful of finely chopped mint
2 tablespoons finely chopped flat parsley
1 tablespoon lemon juice
2 teaspoons olive oil
salt

Cut the lettuce, cucumber and tomato into large chunks and place in a large bowl.

Add the mint and parsley, then pour in the lemon juice and olive oil. Season with salt and toss together well. Serve immediately.

Serves 4

2 small cucumbers
1 Cos lettuce, roughly chopped
2 tomatoes, roughly chopped
1 teaspoon finely chopped hot green chilli
1 teaspoon olive oil
1 tablespoon lemon juice
1 garlic clove, crushed
salt

Cut the cucumbers into quarters lengthways, then chop them widthways.

Place the cucumber pieces in a bowl along with the lettuce, tomatoes and chilli in a bowl. Add the olive oil, lemon juice, garlic and salt to taste and mix together.

Serve with grilled meat or fish.

Making your own yogurt is easy and it's much cheaper than buying it ready-made. It will keep in the fridge for about a week and is used for several other dishes in this book; *salatah khiar bi laban* (yogurt with cucumber dip) (see recipe on page 26), *laban imoo* (lamb with meat) (see recipe on page 93) and *laban ayran* (yogurt drink) (see recipe on page 154). *Laban* is also served alongside other mezze.

Labneh can be made by putting *laban* in cheesecloth or muslin and leaving it to drain overnight. This makes a thicker yogurt and is served with *manakeish bil zahtar* and *manakeish bil jibneh* for breakfast (see recipes on pages 169–170).

Makes 2kg

2 litres full-fat milk
2 tablespoons plain yogurt

Pour the milk into a pan and bring to the boil. Simmer over a medium heat for 10 minutes, then set aside to cool - about 30 minutes.

Add the yogurt to the milk and stir well. Cover the pan with a lid and then wrap it up well in a blanket. Set aside in a warm place for 6 hours.

Remove the lid and place the pan in the fridge for 2 hours before serving.

This recipe makes a large batch of hummus, which will keep for one week in the fridge. The bicarbonate of soda helps the chick peas to cook quickly and also helps loosen their skins so they can be easily removed. Just make sure you rinse the chick peas well after cooking to get rid of any traces of the bicarb. Once refrigerated, the hummus thickens, so make it quite thin to start with. The ice is used to keep the food-processor cool.

Buy good-quality tahini. Good tahini shouldn't taste too bitter. The cheaper brands use peanuts and don't taste good.

Serves 4

500g dried chick peas, soaked overnight and rinsed thoroughly
2 tablespoons bicarbonate of soda
salt
100g ice
200g tahini
4 tablespoons lemon juice

Place the chick peas in a large pan with plenty of fresh cold water and the bicarbonate of soda. Bring to the boil and simmer for about 45 minutes until soft to the touch. Remove the pan from the heat and stir well to loosen the skins from the chick peas. Drain away the water and skins so you are just left with the chick peas. Rinse thoroughly.

Place the chick peas in a food-processor and whizz with a little salt to a smooth purée.

Add the ice, tahini and some of the lemon juice. Whizz again, adding about 500ml of water in a steady stream, until the mixture is smooth and the consistency of a creamy paste. Pour in the remaining lemon juice and add more salt to taste.

متبل باذنجان

moutabal
smoky aubergine dip

Also known as *baba ghanoush* in Syria and Egypt. Charring the aubergines on a gas flame or charcoal grill gives the dip a distinctive smoky flavour. Be careful not to overdo the tahini; you only need a little to bring out the flavour of the aubergines.

Serves 4

2 large aubergines
50g tahini
1 tablespoon lemon juice
salt
olive oil, to drizzle
1 tablespoon pomegranate seeds (optional)

Char the aubergines directly over a gas flame or over charcoal, using tongs, until the flesh is tender. Peel under a cold tap and discard the skins. Allow the aubergines to cool to room temperature.

Finely chop the aubergines and place in a bowl. Add the tahini, lemon juice and salt to taste, and mix well.

Drizzle a little olive oil on top and sprinkle with pomegranate seeds, if using.

محمرة بالجوز

Serves 6

vegetable oil, for deep-frying
50g pistachio nuts
100g walnuts
50g cashew nuts
50g blanched almonds
50g pine nuts (optional)
2 tablespoons finely chopped onion
1 red pepper, finely chopped
1 tablespoon finely chopped flat parsley
150g breadcrumbs
1 green chilli, finely chopped (or 2 teaspoons chilli powder)
250ml olive oil
salt and black pepper

Heat the oil in a deep-fat fryer or deep, heavy-based saucepan. Deep-fry the nuts for a matter of minutes - any longer and the walnuts will taste bitter. Drain and set aside to cool.

Finely chop the nuts and place in a bowl with the onion, red pepper, parsley, breadcrumbs, chilli and olive oil. Season with salt and pepper and mix well. Serve.

fattoush
toasted bread salad

Fattoush is a classic Lebanese dish. It is often eaten by itself as a starter or light lunch. Sumac is an essential ingredient. It is a spice that is made from the dried, powdered berries of the sumac tree.

Serves 4

1 carrot, chopped
1/2 Cos lettuce, chopped
1 cucumber, chopped
2 tomatoes, chopped
5 radishes, chopped
1 tablespoon chopped spring onion
1 red pepper, chopped
1 garlic clove, crushed
1 tablespoon chopped flat parsley
2 teaspoons sumac
1 large flatbread, toasted and broken into pieces
2–3 tablespoons olive oil
salt

Combine all the vegetables in a large bowl and mix well. Add the garlic, parsley, sumac, bread, olive oil and salt to taste. Toss everything together and serve immediately.

foul moukala
broad beans with
garlic and coriander

فول مقلى

I use frozen broad beans for this recipe; they give a better texture than fresh. Wait until the beans are cooled before mixing with the garlic – you'll preserve the garlic's splendour this way.

Serves 4

500g shelled broad beans
1 teaspoon crushed garlic
2 tablespoons chopped coriander
2 tablespoons olive oil
salt and black pepper

Bring the beans to the boil, then simmer for 30 minutes until tender. Drain and set aside to cool.

Place the beans in a bowl with the garlic, coriander, olive oil, salt and pepper. Mix well and serve.

fouter moukala
fried mushrooms with
garlic and coriander

فطر مقلى

Serves 4

vegetable oil, for deep-frying
500g mushrooms, thinly sliced
1 tablespoon olive oil
1 teaspoon crushed garlic
2 tablespoons chopped coriander leaves
salt and black pepper
1/2 teaspoon ground coriander

Heat the vegetable oil in a deep-fat fryer or deep, heavy-based saucepan. Add the mushrooms and fry for about 10 minutes, stirring occasionally, until golden brown and crisp. Remove with a slotted spoon and set aside.

Heat the olive oil in a pan over a low heat. Add the garlic and coriander and cook, stirring, for 10 minutes. Add the fried mushrooms, salt, pepper and ground coriander and stir together. Serve hot or cold.

batinjan makdous
pickled aubergines

My wife's mother makes the best *batinjan makdous*. She does big batches of 15kg aubergines at a time to keep for the year and we always bring home a few jars after we've visited. As they keep for a long time (at least two months), it's worth making a big batch. You will need a few large jars with airtight lids. See picture on page 40.

1kg small aubergines (about 15–20), stalks removed
200g walnuts, finely chopped
1 teaspoon finely chopped green chilli
2 small green peppers, finely chopped
2 small red peppers, finely chopped
4 garlic cloves, finely chopped
salt
plenty of olive oil

Place the aubergines in a large pan, cover with water and bring to the boil. Cook for approximately 20 minutes or until soft but still holding their shape. Drain and drop immediately into a pan of cold water to cool. Drain and set aside.

In a bowl, mix together the walnuts, chilli, peppers, garlic and a pinch of salt.

Make a slit lengthways (not quite end to end) in each aubergine, cutting halfway down the vegetable. Place a little stuffing inside the aubergine. Repeat until all the aubergines are stuffed, then tightly pack the aubergines in glass jars, filling right to the top.

Turn each jar over a sieve to drain any excess liquid and leave overnight.

Pour enough olive oil into each jar to cover the aubergines. They will be ready to serve after 3 weeks.

Lebanese seven spice, or *sabaa baharat*, is a combination of cloves, cumin, nutmeg, coriander, cinnamon and pepper with paprika often added for colour. It can be bought in Mediterranean or Middle Eastern stores.

200g pudding rice
3 medium tomatoes, chopped
2 onions, chopped
half a bunch of flat parsley, chopped
1 tablespoon chopped mint
3 tablespoons lemon juice
150ml olive oil
salt
$1/2$ teaspoon Lebanese seven spice mix (see page 98)
10 small aubergines, stalks removed
4 medium potatoes, sliced into 2cm-thick rounds

Place the rice in a bowl with the tomatoes, onions, parsley and mint. Add the lemon juice, 3 tablespoons of the olive oil, plus the salt and spice mix and mix well.

Hollow out the aubergines using an apple corer, then stuff the aubergines with the rice mixture.

Place the potato slices in the bottom of a saucepan large enough to hold the potato slices in one layer. Lay the stuffed aubergines on top in one layer and pour in the remaining olive oil and enough water to cover the aubergines by a few centimetres. Take a heavy plate just large enough to fit inside the pan and press down - this stops the aubergines from floating around. Place extra weight on the plate if needed.

Bring to the boil, then reduce the heat and cook for about $1^{1/2}$ hours.

Remove the aubergines and leave to cool (use the potatoes for another dish). Serve cold.

market

Oranges, lemons and bananas are some of Lebanon's exports. My father goes every day to these markets to buy fruits and vegetables. These days when you place an order you can find grocers who will prepare your vegetables – chop parsley, hollow out courgettes, peel carrots and take the Jew's mallow leaves off the stem and put them in a bag for you. You can go back in an hour and everything is ready. Of course, they charge more but it saves a lot of time.

Above: a traditional grocery shop with a hairdresser on the right. You can find these shops in every quarter in Beirut because we don't have many big supermarkets. You can also see the word *safa* on the walls – this is a football team in the mountains.

Right: spices for sale – from top left going clockwise: *falafel* spices, turmeric, *kebseh* spices, *frakeh* spices, cinnamon and paprika. The spice in the bottom left looks like *zahtar,* but is, in fact, a spice mix that is used in *frakeh,* a traditional dish from the south of Lebanon that my mother often makes, which is based around raw lamb. *Kebseh* is a dish made with chicken or lamb together with rice.

باذنجان راهب

batinjan rahib
aubergine salad

Some people serve this salad hot, but I think the charred aubergines taste better once cooled.

Serves 4

2 medium aubergines
2 medium tomatoes, finely chopped
1 tablespoon finely chopped onion
1 tablespoon chopped flat parsley
1 garlic clove, crushed
1 tablespoon finely chopped walnuts
1 tablespoon lemon juice
1/2 tablespoon olive oil
salt
1 tablespoon pomegranate seeds (optional)

Char the aubergines directly over a gas flame until the flesh is tender. Peel the skins under a cool tap and discard. Allow the aubergines to cool to room temperature, then finely chop them.

Put the tomatoes, onion and parsley in a bowl and combine with the aubergines, garlic, walnuts, lemon juice, olive oil and salt to taste.

Mix all the ingredients and top with pomegranate seeds, if using. Serve immediately.

tabbouleh
parsley salad
تبولة

Use fine bulgur wheat if you can get it. If not, use regular bulgur wheat. Remember, this is a parsley salad, so parsley should be the main ingredient.

Serves 4

1 tablespoon fine bulgur wheat
1 tablespoon finely chopped onion
juice of 2 lemons
4 tablespoons olive oil
4 tomatoes, finely chopped
200g flat parsley, finely chopped
1 tablespoon finely chopped mint leaves
salt and black pepper

Soak the bulgur wheat in a little cold water for 5 minutes to soften. Place in a bowl with the onion, lemon juice, olive oil, tomatoes, parsley and mint - the bulgur wheat will soak up the other juices in the salad.

Add salt and pepper to taste and serve.

You can buy vine leaves in brine from most supermarkets.

Serves 4

250g pudding rice, rinsed
2 tablespoons finely chopped mint
2 medium onions, finely chopped
5 medium tomatoes, finely chopped
a bunch of flat parsley, finely chopped
4 tablespoons lemon juice
50g olive oil
salt and Lebanese seven spice mix (see page 98)
1 x 250g jar of vine leaves, rinsed
2 medium potatoes, peeled and sliced into rounds

Mix the rice in a bowl with the mint, onions, tomatoes and parsley, then add the lemon juice, olive oil, salt and Lebanese seven spice mix. Place the mixture in a sieve over a bowl and leave to drain for 10–15 minutes. Reserve the liquid.

Lay the vine leaves out on a board. Place a tablespoon of the stuffing near the stem end of each vine leaf. Fold the bottom and sides of the leaf over the stuffing and roll up firmly to give a cigar shape. Repeat with the other vine leaves.

Place the potato rounds in the bottom of a large, heavy-based pan and pack the stuffed vine leaves closely together on top, in layers.

Put a heavy plate that fits inside the pan on top, to keep the rolls in shape during cooking. Place a heatproof bowl filled with water on top to add extra weight. Pour in the reserved liquid and enough water to cover the plate by a few centimetres.

Cover with a lid and bring to the boil, then reduce the heat and cook very gently for $1^1/_2$ hours.

Drain the liquid from the pan. Serve the vine leaves cold with *laban* (yogurt) (see recipe on page 34) and with the cooked potatoes too, if you wish.

لوبية بالزيت

loubia bi zeit
green beans in oil

Serves 4

3 tablespoons olive oil
1/2 onion, finely chopped
3 garlic cloves, chopped
500g green beans, cut into three pieces
5 ripe tomatoes, chopped
1 tablespoon tomato purée, mixed in 350ml water
salt and black pepper

Heat the olive oil in a saucepan and fry the onion and garlic until softened. Add the green beans and cook for 5 minutes, stirring occasionally.

Add the tomatoes and stir occasionally until tender. Stir in the tomato purée mixture and salt and pepper to taste. Bring the mixture to the boil, then cook over a low heat for 45 minutes.

Serve cold with spring onions.

فاصوليا بالزيت

fasoulieh bi zeit
beans in oil

Serves 4

150g dried cannellini beans
1 tablespoon lemon juice
1 teaspoon crushed garlic
salt
2 tablespoons olive oil

Soak the beans overnight in cold water. Drain and rinse, then place in a pan. Cover with cold water and bring to the boil. Simmer for about 30 minutes or until cooked, then drain and set aside to cool.

Transfer the beans to a serving dish and toss with the remainder of the ingredients. Mix well and serve.

We also use the name *asoura* for this dish, which means 'squeezed' – this is what you do with the chicory.

Serves 4

300g chicory, roughly chopped
olive oil
lemon juice
salt

Bring the chicory to the boil in a pan full of water. Boil for 15 minutes or until soft. Drain and set aside to cool.

Squeeze out the water with your hands until the chicory is dry. Form into balls about 6cm wide. At this stage you can put the chicory in the fridge - it will keep for about a week like this.

When ready to serve, place a ball on a plate, flatten out and drizzle with olive oil and lemon juice. Season with salt to taste.

moussaka bi zeit
aubergine and tomato moussaka

This is one of my favourite dishes. It's a traditional and easy recipe, one that I always cook for vegetarians. The aubergines are cooked twice, giving them lots of flavour.

Serves 4

3–4 aubergines
vegetable oil, for deep-frying
225g cooked chick peas
100ml olive oil
6 garlic cloves, finely sliced
1 onion, finely sliced
2 x 440g tins of chopped tomatoes
2 tablespoons tomato purée
salt and black pepper
2 large tomatoes, sliced

Preheat the oven to 180°C/350°F/gas mark 4.

Peel the aubergines lengthways with a potato peeler, leaving long stripes of skin. Cut each one in half widthways and then slice the two halves lengthways.

Heat the oil in a deep-fat fryer or deep, heavy-based saucepan. Deep-fry the aubergine slices until browned. Remove with a slotted spoon and spread out in a deep ovenproof tray in one layer. Spread the chick peas on top of the aubergine slices.

Heat the olive oil separately and cook the garlic and onion until softened. Add the chopped tomatoes, the tomato purée and salt and pepper to taste. Stir and cook over a low heat for 30 minutes.

Pour the tomato mixture over the chick peas. Arrange the sliced tomatoes over the top, then bake in the oven for 30 minutes. Cut into pieces and serve cold, or hot with rice.

barassia
leeks in oil

Serves 4

500g leeks, cut into chunks
3 tablespoons olive oil
3 garlic cloves, crushed
1 tablespoon chopped coriander
salt and black pepper

Bring a pan of water to the boil and cook the leeks for 15 minutes or until tender. Drain and set aside to cool.

Heat the olive oil in a pan and gently cook the garlic until softened. Add the coriander, salt and pepper and cook for a few more minutes, stirring. Add this mixture to the leeks and mix well. Serve immediately.

بامية بالزيت

bamia bi zeit
okra in oil

Use baby okra which are 1–3cm long and can be bought frozen.

Serves 4

vegetable oil, for deep-frying
500g baby okra
3 tablespoons olive oil
1/2 onion, finely chopped
5 garlic cloves, crushed
5–6 ripe tomatoes, chopped
2 tablespoons tomato purée, mixed in 250ml water
salt and black pepper
a large handful of coriander, chopped

Heat the oil in a deep-fat fryer or deep, heavy-based saucepan. Deep-fry the okra until browned. Set aside to cool.

Heat the olive oil in a pan, then add the onion and garlic and stir occasionally until browned. Add the tomatoes and cook over a medium heat until tender, then add the tomato purée mixture and salt and pepper to taste. Cook for 20 minutes, then stir through the coriander and cook over a low heat for a further 15 minutes. Stir in the okra and set aside to cool. Serve cold.

سلق بالزيت

Serves 4

for the stuffing
250g pudding rice, rinsed
2 onions, chopped
5 medium tomatoes, chopped
2 handfuls of flat parsley, chopped
100g cooked chick peas
3 tablespoons lemon juice
3–4 tablespoons olive oil
salt and black pepper

1.5kg Swiss chard
3 tablespoons olive oil

For the stuffing, place the rice in a bowl with the other stuffing ingredients. Mix together and transfer to a sieve placed over a bowl to catch the mixture's juices. Drain for about 15 minutes.

Cut off the stalk ends of the Swiss chard and place them in a deep saucepan (this is to protect the leaves from burning during cooking). Drop the leaves into a pan of boiling water. Blanch for a minute or two, then drain and leave to cool slightly.

Lay out the Swiss chard leaves on a board. Put 1 tablespoon of the stuffing on each leaf, tuck in the ends and roll up firmly.

Place the filled leaves in the pan on the top of the stalk ends. Cover with a heavy plate that fits inside the pan (this packs the stuffed leaves down so they hold their shape). Add the reserved soaking juice and olive oil to the pan and pour in enough water to cover the plate by a few centimetres. Bring to the boil, then reduce the heat to very low and cook for 1^1/$_2$ hours.

Drain the stuffed leaves and discard the stalks. Serve cold with *laban* (yogurt) (see recipe on page 34).

foul medames

fava beans with garlic and chick peas

We usually eat this for breakfast with yogurt, soft cheese and olives. It is quite filling and you'll find you don't need lunch! If you are short of time, use two tins of fava beans and one tin of chick peas instead of dried.

Serves 4

200g dried fava beans
100g dried chick peas
1 teaspoon bicarbonate of soda
2 garlic cloves, crushed
juice of 2 lemons
1 teaspoon ground cumin
salt
olive oil
1 tablespoon chopped parsley

Soak the fava beans and chick peas in separate bowls for 8 hours or overnight.

Drain the fava beans, rinse and place in a saucepan. Cover with water and bring to the boil. Cook for about 45 minutes or until tender.

Meanwhile, bring a separate pan of water to the boil and add the bicarbonate of soda and drained chick peas. Cook for about 40 minutes or until tender. Rinse under cold water to remove the bicarbonate of soda, then boil again in fresh water for a further 5 minutes. Drain.

Drain the fava beans and place in a bowl with the chick peas. Roughly mash with a spoon or pestle, then add the garlic, lemon juice, cumin and salt to taste. Mix well.

Transfer to a serving dish and finish with olive oil and parsley. Serve with lettuce, tomatoes, spring onions, radishes and pickles.

When boiling the chick peas, ensure you don't cook them for too long. They should be soft but still holding their shape.

Serves 4

100g dried chick peas
1 teaspoon bicarbonate of soda
1 teaspoon crushed garlic
salt
cumin
olive oil

Soak the chick peas for 8 hours or overnight.

Drain the chick peas and place in a saucepan. Cover with water, add the bicarbonate of soda and bring to the boil. Cook for about 45 minutes or until the chick peas are soft. Drain and rinse well to get rid of the bicarbonate of soda.

Place the chick peas back in the pan and cover with water. Bring back to the boil, then drain and place in a bowl with the garlic, and salt and cumin to taste. Mix well. Transfer to a serving dish and pour olive oil on top.

Serve with pickles or fresh raw vegetables such as tomatoes, radishes and spring onions.

Hummus snouber is also popular – follow the same recipe but omit the lamb.

Serves 4

1 quantity *hummus bil tahina* (see recipe on page 35)
1 tablespoon vegetable oil
100g lamb shoulder, cut into 1cm pieces
1 teaspoon pine nuts
salt and black pepper

Place the hummus in a serving dish and use a tablespoon to make a well in the centre.

Heat the vegetable oil in a frying pan and fry the lamb and pine nuts for 5–7 minutes. Stir well, then add salt and pepper and cook until the meat is tender.

Arrange the meat and pine nuts in the well of the hummus and sprinkle with more black pepper.

moujadara
lentils and rice with crispy onions

This is always a favourite at my restaurant, Le Mignon. You can use either brown or green lentils, but I find that brown lentils give a much better result.

Serves 4

225g brown or green dried lentils, rinsed
4 tablespoons olive oil
1/2 small onion, finely chopped
100g basmati rice
salt and black pepper
1 teaspoon cumin

for the crispy onions
vegetable oil
4 tablespoons sliced onion

Place the lentils in a deep pan, cover with water and bring to the boil. Boil for 20 minutes, then drain and set aside.

Heat the olive oil in a pan, add the chopped onion and fry until browned. Add the rice, cooked lentils, salt, pepper and cumin and just enough water to cover. Cover and bring to the boil, then reduce the heat and stir occasionally for 15 minutes or until the rice is cooked. Place in a serving dish.

For the crispy onions, pour vegetable oil into a deep frying pan to the depth of about 5cm. Heat well and deep-fry the sliced onion until brown and crispy. Remove from the pan and arrange on top of the lentil and rice mixture. Serve hot.

Unlike the spinach and cheese pastries, these meat pastries shouldn't be baked in the oven – they are best deep-fried. They can be stored in the freezer for up to 3 weeks.

Serves 4 plus extra for freezing

for the stuffing
2 tablespoons vegetable oil
300g minced lamb
1 medium onion, chopped
100g pine nuts
salt and black pepper
1 teaspoon cinnamon
50g *labneh* (see recipe on page 34)
1 tablespoon finely chopped flat parsley

500g pastry dough (see recipe on page 138)
flour, for dusting
vegetable oil, for deep-frying

Start by preparing the stuffing. Heat the oil in a pan and cook the lamb, stirring occasionally, until browned. Add the onion, pine nuts, salt, pepper and cinnamon and cook for a further 25 minutes. Spread out in a large tray so that the mixture cools quickly.

When the meat mixture has cooled, transfer to a bowl and add the labneh and parsley. Mix well.

Roll out the dough on a floured surface to a 2mm thickness. Cut into 10cm rounds with a pastry cutter.

Put $1^1/_2$ teaspoons of the stuffing in the middle of each dough circle. Fold over one side to make semi circles. Seal the edges together using the prongs of a fork and make a pattern around the edge. (The pastries can be frozen at this stage by placing them on a floured baking sheet.)

Heat the oil in a deep-fat fryer or deep, heavy-based saucepan. Slide in the pastries and cook for about 5–7 minutes until golden brown.

Drain and serve hot or cold.

cheese pastries
sambousak jibneh

These pastries can be cooked straight from frozen. Simply place the pastries on a floured baking tray before freezing.

If you don't want to deep-fry, cut the pastry into rectangles, place the stuffing in the centre and pinch the sides to make small boats. Then bake in a moderate oven for about 15 minutes or until golden brown. See picture on page 64.

Serves 4 plus extra for freezing

for the stuffing
300g halloumi or feta cheese, grated
2 tablespoons chopped flat parsley
3 tablespoons butter, melted

500g pastry dough (see recipe on page 138)
flour, for dusting
vegetable oil, for deep-frying

Rinse the halloumi if you find it too salty. Place the halloumi or feta in a bowl, add the parsley and melted butter and mix well until it all sticks together.

Divide the dough into walnut-sized balls. Roll out each ball on a floured surface to a 2mm thickness.

Put a tablespoon or so of stuffing in the middle of each dough circle. Fold in half, corner to corner, and seal well in a crescent shape.

Heat the oil in a deep-fat fryer or deep, heavy-based saucepan. Gently lower the pastries into the hot oil and deep-fry for about 5–10 minutes until golden. Serve hot.

These pastries freeze well so it's a good idea to make a big batch, then you can easily take them out and fry or bake them when needed. Place on a baking tray wiped with vegetable oil or a little flour before freezing. See picture on page 64 – the spinach pastries are the triangular shaped ones at the back.

Serves 8

for the stuffing
1kg fresh spinach, or frozen, thawed
salt and black pepper
2 medium onions, finely chopped
2 tablespoons pine nuts
4 tablespoons sumac
juice of 2 lemons
100ml olive oil

500g pastry dough (see recipe on page 138)
flour, for dusting
vegetable oil, for deep-frying

Wash the spinach well, if using fresh. Finely chop and place in a bowl. Sprinkle with salt and rub well with your hands until soft. Squeeze to drain off excess water. Add the onions, pine nuts, sumac, lemon juice, olive oil, salt and pepper and mix well. Drain the excess liquid to get a thick and dry stuffing.

Roll out the dough on a floured surface to a 2mm thickness. Cut into rounds using a 10cm pastry cutter.

Place a tablespoon of the spinach filling in the middle of each circle. Bring up the edges at 3 points to form a triangular shape. Press the edges firmly together with your fingertips to seal completely.

Heat the vegetable oil in a deep-fat fryer or deep, heavy-based saucepan and deep-fry the pastries for about 5 minutes or until golden brown. Drain, leave to cool slightly and serve warm. Alternatively, bake in a moderate oven for about 10–15 minutes.

manakeish bil zahtar
bread baked with thyme

Manakeish bil zahtar, manakeish bil jibneh and *lahma bi ajeen* (see recipes on pages 70–71) are often eaten for breakfast in Lebanon with black tea. *Zahtar* is a mixture of wild thyme, sumac and toasted sesame seeds. I buy it ready mixed from Lebanon. You can find it in Middle Eastern food stores.

Serves 4

4 tablespoons *zahtar,* with a little extra sumac added
6 tablespoons olive oil, plus extra for greasing
6–8 balls bread dough (see recipe on page 136)
2 tablespoons plain flour

Preheat the oven to 180°C/350°F/gas mark 4.

Place the *zahtar* and olive oil in a bowl and mix. Sprinkle the dough balls with flour, then roll out on a board into flat circular shapes. Place on an oiled baking tray.

Spread a little of the *zahtar* mixture over each piece of dough. Make indents with your fingers all over the dough to stop the bread from puffing up during cooking.

Bake in the oven for about 10 minutes or until the bread is golden brown. Be careful as the *zahtar* burns quite quickly.

Serve with cucumbers, tomatoes, olives and fresh mint.

manakeish bil jibneh
baked dough with cheese

In Lebanon we use a cheese called *akewi*. It's difficult to find in the West, but halloumi or feta work just as well. See picture on page 68.

Serves 4

350g halloumi
6–8 balls bread dough (see recipe on page 138)
2 tablespoons plain flour
1 tablespoon melted butter, plus extra for greasing
1 teaspoon sesame seeds

Preheat the oven to 180°C/350°F/gas mark 4.

Wash the cheese to get rid of the salt. Cut into thin slices.

Sprinkle the dough balls with flour, then roll out into 15cm discs. Place on a greased baking tray.

Brush the butter over the dough using a pastry brush. Divide the slices of cheese between the discs. Sprinkle with sesame seeds, then use your fingers to make indents in the dough – this stops the bread from puffing up in the oven. Bake in the oven for about 10 minutes or until the bread is golden around the edges.

Serve with olives and cucumbers.

Good with *laban* (yogurt) or with *laban ayran* (yogurt drink) (see recipes on pages 34 and 154) for an early lunch. See picture on page 68.

Serves 4

1/4 onion
2 tomatoes
1 small green chilli
150g finely minced lamb
1 tablespoon tomato purée
salt and black pepper
6–8 balls bread dough (see recipe on page 136)
2 tablespoons plain flour
1 teaspoon olive oil, for greasing
1 tablespoon pine nuts

Preheat the oven to 180°C/350°F/gas mark 4.

Whizz the onion, tomatoes and green chilli in a food-processor to a fine paste. Transfer to a bowl and add the mince, tomato purée, salt and pepper and mix well.

Sprinkle the dough balls with flour and roll out into flat circular shapes about 2mm thick. Place the dough circles on an oiled baking tray. Spread some of the meat mixture on each circle, then sprinkle over the pine nuts. Bake in the oven for about 15 minutes. Serve.

Left: this bread is very popular in Lebanon. It is called *ka'ak*. People like to walk along the corniche in Beirut in the evening or afternoon. They buy bread or nuts, and often an espresso as well, and sometimes sit out until late at night. You can buy *ka'ak* at any time of day – and it is much cheaper than going to a restaurant! For breakfast, they put soft cheese inside, so it melts, or you could have it with *zahtar*. It will fill you up for the whole day.

When I go to Lebanon on holiday each year I like to go to a bakery called *abu Arab* in Al-Naameh in the south, by the sea. There you can find the best *ka'ak* in Lebanon. They start making the dough very early in the morning and sell the *ka'ak* all day long. They are huge but I always find I can eat two!

Below: another popular snack is nuts, and you can buy many different kinds and flavours from sellers like this one – pistachios, cashews, peanuts, watermelon seeds, pumpkin seeds, roasted chick peas and barbecued almonds are all on offer, which you can buy with or without salt added. The pink ones in the picture are roasted chick peas covered with sugar, which are very popular with children.

There are lots of shops selling *falafel* in Lebanon and it always makes a good, cheap lunch. Now you can make your own at home.

Serves 4

200g dried broad beans, soaked overnight, then rinsed and drained
100g dried chick peas, soaked overnight, then rinsed and drained
1/2 onion
1/2 red pepper
3 tablespoons roughly chopped coriander
5 garlic cloves
1 teaspoon ground cumin
2 tablespoons ground coriander
1 teaspoon bicarbonate of soda
1 teaspoon sesame seeds
salt and black pepper
vegetable oil, for deep-frying

Whizz the beans and chick peas in a food-processor until very fine. Remove and set aside in a large bowl.

Whizz the onion, pepper, fresh coriander and garlic in the food-processor until fine, then add to the beans and chick peas along with the cumin, ground coriander, bicarbonate of soda, sesame seeds, salt and pepper and mix well with your hands. Add enough water to make a smooth dough and set aside for 15 minutes.

Heat the oil in a deep-fat fryer or deep, heavy-based saucepan. Mould the mixture into balls with your hands or using an ice-cream scoop. Gently lower into the hot oil and fry until browned.

Serve with pitta bread, *tarator* (tahini sauce) (see recipe on page 140), pickles and salad.

Serves 4

vegetable oil, for deep-frying
1kg potatoes, peeled and chopped into 1cm cubes
4 tablespoons olive oil
1/2 onion, finely chopped
1 teaspoon crushed garlic
1 red pepper, finely chopped
2 green chillies, finely chopped
1 tablespoon finely chopped fresh coriander
salt and black pepper
1/2 teaspoon ground coriander

Heat the oil in a deep-fat fryer or deep, heavy-based saucepan. Deep-fry the
potatoes until crisp. Drain and set aside.

Meanwhile, heat the olive oil in a pan and fry the onion, garlic, pepper,
chillies and fresh coriander until softened. Add the potatoes along with salt,
pepper and ground coriander to taste. Stir to combine and serve.

sawda dajaj
fried chicken livers

Serves 2

4 tablespoons vegetable oil, for frying
100g chicken livers
salt and black pepper
juice of ¹/₂ lemon
1 teaspoon pomegranate molasses
1 tablespoon garlic sauce (see recipe on page 140)

Heat the oil over a high heat in a frying pan so it is a couple of centimetres deep. When hot, add the chicken livers and stir continuously until cooked - about 15–20 minutes.

Drain the oil from the pan, then add salt, pepper, the lemon juice, pomegranate molasses and garlic sauce and stir for a couple of minutes.

Serve hot with other starters and toasted bread.

Serves 4

250g finely minced lamb
1 tablespoon finely chopped onion
1 tablespoon finely chopped red pepper
1 tablespoon chopped parsley
salt and black pepper
6 pitta breads
2 tablespoons *tarator* (see recipe on page 140)
1 tablespoon pine nuts

Preheat the grill to low.

Place the mince, onion, pepper and parsley in a bowl. Add salt and pepper to taste and mix well.

Cut open each bread and spread a thin layer of the mince mixture inside. Drizzle in a little *tarator* and add a few pine nuts to each. Close the breads and flatten them, then place under the grill, turning, so as not to burn the bread before the meat is cooked. This should take about 5 minutes. Serve hot.

makloubeh batinjan
aubergine with meat and rice

'Makloubeh' means upside-down – this dish is prepared in a bowl and then turned out on to a plate to give a dome shape. You can use a big bowl as a mould or four smaller ones. One of my favourite aubergine recipes!

Serves 4

4 large aubergines
vegetable oil, for deep-frying
2 tablespoons olive oil
1/2 onion, finely chopped
250g lamb shoulder, chopped into 3cm chunks
300g basmati or American long-grain rice, soaked for 20 minutes
salt and black pepper
200g peeled peanuts, almonds or cashews

Peel the aubergines lengthways with a potato peeler, leaving long stripes of skin. Cut one into cubes and the other three into thin slices.

Heat the vegetable oil in a deep-fat fryer or deep, heavy-based saucepan. Deep-fry the sliced aubergines until browned, then drain and set aside. Repeat with the cubed aubergine.

Heat the olive oil in a pan and fry the onion until softened. Stir in the meat and cook until browned, then add the cubed eggplant and 700ml of water. Cook over a low heat for about 15 minutes until the water colours.

Add the rice, salt and pepper and cook for a further 20 minutes.

Meanwhile, deep-fry the nuts until golden. Drain and place in a serving bowl.

Line a large bowl with the aubergine slices. Pack the rice mixture in firmly, then place a large flat dish on top of the bowl. Turn out the aubergine 'cake', being careful to keep its dome shape.

Serve the bowl of nuts alongside the aubergine cake. Serve with any type of salad.

كبة بالصنية

kibbeh bil sainieh
baked kibbeh

Kibbeh is a traditional Lebanese dish with several variations. Fine bulgur wheat is mixed with ground meat and spices, as below, or with potato, (kibbeh batata) and cooked. Kibbeh nayeh is the version made with raw meat.

Serves 6

for the stuffing
2 tablespoons vegetable oil
1 onion, finely chopped
250g minced lamb
2 tablespoons pine nuts
salt and black pepper
1/2 teaspoon cinnamon

for the dough
500g fine bulgur wheat, soaked in water for about 15 minutes, then drained
500g lean minced lamb
salt
1 teaspoon kibbeh spices (available ready-mixed from Middle Eastern
   stores, or use a mixture of cumin, black pepper and salt)

1 medium onion
3 teaspoons ghee (clarified butter)

Preheat the oven to 180°C/350°F/gas mark 4.

Prepare the stuffing first. Heat the oil in a saucepan and add the onion. Cook, stirring, until softened. Add the meat and cook until browned. Add the pine nuts, salt, pepper and cinnamon and cook for a further 15 minutes, stirring all the time. Set aside to cool.

Next prepare the kibbeh dough. Whizz the meat in a food-processor until smooth. Add the meat to the bulgur wheat along with the salt and spices. Whizz the onion in the food-processor until fine, then add to the meat mixture. Mix well until it all sticks together.

Use some of the ghee to grease a large baking tray with a lip and spread half of the kibbeh dough in the tray in an even layer. Wet your hands and smooth the surface. Spread the stuffing over in another layer, then finish with another layer of the dough. Use a knife to cut the kibbeh into small squares, keeping them in the tray. Dot over the remaining ghee.

Place the tray in the oven and cook for 30 minutes. Serve with *laban* (yogurt) or *salatah khiar bi laban* (cucumber salad) (see recipes on pages 34 and 28).

You can prepare this kofta in one big slice as per page 84, but it is nicer to do them in individual patties as below.

Serves 4

500g minced lamb
$1/2$ onion, finely chopped
1 medium red pepper, finely chopped
2 tablespoons finely chopped parsley
salt and black pepper
vegetable oil, for deep-frying
2 medium aubergines, peeled
2 tablespoons tomato purée, mixed in 400ml water

Preheat the oven to 180°C/350°F/gas mark 4.

Place the minced lamb in a bowl and add the onion, red pepper, parsley, salt and pepper. Mix all the ingredients together, then mould into 10cm square patties about 1cm deep. Place on baking trays and bake in the oven for 10 minutes.

Heat the oil in a deep-fat fryer or deep, heavy-based saucepan. Slice the aubergines into rounds and deep-fry until browned, then drain and set aside.

Remove the trays from the oven and drain any excess oil. Pour the tomato purée mixture over the patties and place an aubergine slice on each one. Return the trays to the oven for 30 minutes or until the sauce has thickened.

Serve hot with *roz abiad* (white rice) or *roz bil sha'rieh* (rice with vermicelli) (see recipes on pages 138 and 139).

kofta bil tahina
kofta with tahini

كفتة بالطحينة

Serves 4

500g minced lamb
$1/2$ medium onion, finely chopped
1 tablespoon finely chopped parsley
salt and black pepper
150ml tahini sauce (see recipe on page 140)
50g pine nuts

Preheat the oven to 180°C/350°F/gas mark 4.

Place the meat in a bowl with the onion, parsley, salt and pepper. Mix all the ingredients until the mixture holds together.

Spread the mixture evenly in a baking tray. Cook for 15 minutes in the oven, then remove and drain the excess fat. Spread the tahini sauce over the top and sprinkle over the pine nuts. Return the tray to the oven for a further 15 minutes until the pine nuts are golden.

Cut into squares and serve hot alongside raw vegetables or salads.

Serves 4

2 tablespoons olive oil
300g lamb shoulder, cut into large pieces
200g shelled broad beans
200g American long-grain rice, soaked for 20 minutes and drained
salt and black pepper

Heat the olive oil in a pan and add the lamb. Cook over a moderate heat for 15 minutes until the meat is tender.

Add the beans to the pan and cook for 5 minutes. Stir in the rice, along with 600ml of water, salt and pepper.

Bring to the boil, then reduce the heat and cook for 15 minutes or until the rice has absorbed all the liquid.

Turn into a serving platter and serve with *laban* (yogurt) (see recipe on page 34).

koosa wa warak einab mahshi
stuffed courgettes and vine leaves
كوسى ورق عنب محشي

This is a meal in one. All you need is some *laban* (yogurt) (see recipe on page 34) to serve on the side.

Serves 4

8 small courgettes
150g pudding rice
200g minced lamb
1 tablespoon ghee (clarified butter)
salt and black pepper
20 vine leaves (you can buy these in a jar from the supermarket)
6–7 lamb cutlets
juice of 3 lemons

Cut the stems off the courgettes and hollow each one out using an apple corer. Rinse well.

Wash and drain the rice and place in a bowl. Add the mince, ghee, salt and pepper and mix well.

Use the rice mixture to stuff each courgette until it is three-quarters full, reserving some of the mixture for the vine leaves. Set aside.

Spread the vine leaves out on a plate, put a little stuffing in the centre of each, tuck in the sides and roll up to make cigar shapes.

Place the lamb cutlets in one layer in the bottom of a large saucepan. Arrange the stuffed vine leaves in a ring in a tightly packed layer and place the stuffed courgettes in the middle. Use a plate that just fits inside the pan to press on top. Place a bowl of water on the plate to weigh it down. Pour in enough water to cover by about 5cm and squeeze in the lemon juice. Bring to the boil, then reduce the heat and cook for about $1^{1/2}$ hours. Drain.

Arrange the stuffed vine leaves and courgettes on a serving platter and serve hot.

koosa wa batinjan mahshi bil banadorah
stuffed courgettes and aubergines in tomato sauce

Serves 4

6 small courgettes
6 small aubergines
200g pudding rice, rinsed
200g minced lamb
2 tablespoons ghee (clarified butter)
salt and black pepper
4 tablespoons tomato purée, mixed in 1 litre water
1 teaspoon dried mint

Cut the stems off the courgettes and hollow out with an apple corer. Rinse well. Do the same with the aubergines.

Place the rice in a bowl with the mince, ghee, salt and pepper. Mix well.

Stuff each courgette and aubergine with the rice mixture until three-quarters full. It's best to do this with your hands. Place in a large saucepan.

Pour in the tomato purée mixture, the dried mint and some salt. Use a plate that just fits inside the pan to push down on top of the stuffed vegetables. Place a bowl of water on top to weigh it down. Bring to the boil over a medium heat, then reduce the heat and cook gently for 1 hour.

Remove the stuffed vegetables from the pan and transfer to a serving bowl. Pour over any remaining tomato sauce. Serve hot.

كوسى بالأبلمة

koosa bil ablama
stuffed courgettes

Use the smaller-sized courgettes for this recipe. The western ones will be too big to stuff. Instead of throwing away the courgette pulp try cooking it up with scrambled eggs – delicious!

Serves 4

8–12 courgettes, stems trimmed
100ml vegetable oil, plus an extra 2 tablespoons
1 medium onion, chopped
500g minced lamb
1 tablespoon pine nuts
salt and black pepper
3 tablespoons tomato purée, mixed in 1 litre water

Hollow out the courgettes at the stem end using an apple corer (see picture below) – keep the pulp to use later or simply discard.

Heat the 100ml of vegetable oil in a deep frying pan and fry the courgettes for 5 minutes on each side until browned (you may need to do this in batches). Drain and set aside to cool.

Meanwhile, heat the 2 tablespoons of oil in another pan. Add the onion and cook, stirring, until softened. Add the lamb, pine nuts and salt and pepper. Stir well until the meat is browned, then remove the pan from the heat.

Stuff each courgette with the mixture until three-quarters full. Set aside.

Pour the tomato purée mixture into a pan and season with salt and pepper. Bring to the boil, then reduce the heat and add the stuffed courgettes. Cook over a low heat for 25 minutes.

Serve with *roz abiad* (white rice) (see recipe on page 138).

frikkeh bil lahma
roasted green wheat with lamb

Frikkeh is roasted green wheat (see picture below) and it is a speciality of Lebanon. It has a delicious taste. You can do this dish with chicken instead of lamb if you prefer.

Serves 4

250g roasted green wheat
300g lamb shoulder, cut into large pieces
2 tablespoons ghee (clarified butter)
1 medium onion, chopped
salt
200g nuts (such as pine nuts, cashews and blanched almonds),
   toasted until golden

Soak the wheat in a bowl of cold water for 30 minutes. Skim off the dust that floats to the top and rinse in several changes of fresh water. Drain and set aside.

Meanwhile, bring a pan of water to the boil, add the lamb and cook until tender – this will take about 25 minutes. Drain, reserving the cooking water.

Heat the ghee in a separate pan, add the onion and cook until softened. Add the drained wheat and some salt and cook for 5 minutes, stirring.

Pour about 400ml of the reserved cooking water into the pan, bring to the boil, then reduce the heat and cook gently for 45 minutes until the wheat is tender but still has a bit of bite.

Divide the wheat between serving plates. Arrange the cooked meat on top and scatter with the toasted nuts.

Serve with *laban* (yogurt) or *salatah lebnanieh* (Lebanese salad) (see recipes on pages 34 and 31).

burghul bil lahma
bulgur wheat with lamb

Serves 6

2 tablespoons olive oil
2 tablespoons finely chopped onion
100g lamb shoulder, cut into chunks
250g coarse bulgur wheat
salt and black pepper
50g cooked chick peas

Heat the olive oil in a pan, add the onion and stir until softened. Add the lamb and cook for 15 minutes until browned.

Stir in the bulgur wheat, salt, pepper and 500ml of water. Finally add the chickpeas and bring to the boil. Reduce the heat and simmer for 30 minutes, or until the bulgur wheat is cooked.

Serve with *laban* (yogurt) (see recipe on page 34) and salads.

lamb

All main courses in Lebanon revolve around meat. Beef is the meat that is most commonly eaten at home, because it is cheaper than lamb. The fat-tailed sheep that are native to Lebanon are expensive because they are organically reared – it is actually cheaper to buy imported lamb from New Zealand. Personally I prefer lamb and as it is cheaper than beef in the UK I use it in all my main courses. I always mince my own lamb so that I know it will be of good quality.

The fatty tail of the fat-tailed sheep is a delicacy and is used in *kibbeh nayeh* – a very traditional recipe made with raw meat together with fresh basil and mint to add flavour. The fat is also threaded on to kebabs with chunks of meat.

Serves 4

300g lamb shoulder, cut into large chunks
1 large onion, roughly chopped
1kg yogurt (see recipe on page 34)
1 egg
salt and black pepper
2 tablespoons cornflour

Place the meat in a pan with the chopped onion. Add 500ml of water
and bring to the boil. Skim off any scum that floats to the top and continue
simmering and skimming until the liquid is clear – this will take 10-15
minutes. Drain the meat and onion and set aside.

Pour the yogurt into a large saucepan with the egg, salt and pepper and beat
well. Add the water the meat was cooked in and place over a medium heat.
Bring to the boil, stirring all the time with a balloon whisk to keep it smooth.

Mix the cornflour with a little water, add to the pan and whisk well. Reduce
the heat and simmer for 30 minutes. Add the boiled meat and onion and
simmer for a further 20 minutes.

Serve hot with *roz abiad* (white rice) (see recipe on page 138).

سبانخ باللحمة

sabanikh wa roz
spinach with rice

Serves 4

3 tablespoons vegetable oil
3 garlic cloves, chopped
1 onion, finely chopped
200g coriander, chopped
50g pine nuts
200g lamb shoulder, chopped into $^1/_2$–1cm pieces – get your butcher
  to prepare this for you
salt
500g spinach, washed and finely chopped
juice of 1 lemon, or to taste

Heat the vegetable oil in a pan, add the garlic and onion and stir until
tender. Add the coriander and mix well. Add the pine nuts and meat and
stir occasionally until the meat is tender.

Season with salt and add the spinach to the pan and stir together for
5 minutes. Pour in enough water to cover, bring to the boil and cook over
a moderate heat for 30 minutes.

Turn into a serving platter, and squeeze over the lemon juice.

Serve hot with *roz abiad* (white rice) (see recipe on page 138).

moujadara hamra
lentils with bulgur wheat

This dish is from the south of Lebanon.

Serves 6

250g brown lentils
4 tablespoons olive oil
4 tablespoons vegetable oil
4 large onions, chopped
150g bulgur wheat
salt

Bring a pan of water to the boil and par-boil the lentils for 15-20 minutes. Drain and set aside.

Heat the olive oil and vegetable oil in a pan. Add the onions and fry until well browned, stirring all the time. Add 500ml of water, bring to the boil and simmer for 15–20 minutes until the water has taken on the colour from the onions.

Add the lentils, bulgur wheat and salt. Cover with a lid, reduce the heat and cook for about 20 minutes until the lentils and bulgur wheat are tender.

Serve hot or cold with yogurt and pickles or salad.

ardishawki bil lahma

artichoke hearts with lamb

Serves 4

8 artichoke hearts, frozen or from a jar
2 tablespoons olive oil
2 tablespoons finely chopped onion
200g minced lamb
1 tablespoon finely chopped red pepper
1 tablespoon finely chopped green pepper
salt and black pepper
3 medium tomatoes, sliced
2 tablespoons tomato purée, mixed in 300ml water

Preheat the oven to 180°C/350°F/gas mark 4.

Boil the frozen artichoke hearts in a pan for 15 minutes, then drain. If using jarred artichokes, boil for a couple of minutes, then drain.

Heat the olive oil in a saucepan, add the onion and cook until tender. Add the mince and cook for 5 minutes, stirring occasionally. Add the red and green pepper, salt and pepper and cook for a further 10 minutes until softened. Remove from the heat.

Place the artichoke hearts in a deep baking tray. Put a tablespoon of the mince mixture on top of each artichoke and top with a tomato slice. Pour the tomato purée mixture around the artichokes and season with extra salt. Bake in the oven for 30 minutes. Serve with *roz abiad* (white rice) (see recipe on page 138).

Serves 6

4 tablespoons olive oil
1/2 onion, chopped
7 garlic cloves, crushed
500g lamb shoulder, cut into large pieces
6 medium tomatoes, finely chopped
2 tablespoons tomato purée, mixed in 500ml water
salt and black pepper
a large handful of coriander, chopped
1kg okra (frozen is best)
juice of 1 lemon (optional)

Heat the olive oil in a pan, add the onion and garlic and stir until softened.
Add the lamb and cook until browned, stirring occasionally. Stir in the
tomatoes and cook over a low heat for 5 minutes.

Pour in the tomato purée mixture, salt and pepper and bring to the boil,
then reduce the heat. Add the coriander and okra and cook for a further
25 minutes.

Squeeze over a little lemon juice if you wish, and serve with *roz abiad* (white
rice) (see recipe on page 138).

stuffed baked vegetables
khoudar mahshi bil forn

Lebanese seven spice, or *sabaa baharat*, is a spice mix of cloves, cumin, nutmeg, coriander, cinnamon, pepper and paprika. It can be bought in Middle Eastern stores.

Serves 6

1 tablespoon olive oil
2 tablespoons chopped onions
300g minced lamb
salt and black pepper
1 teaspoon Lebanese seven spice mix
1 tablespoon pine nuts
4 tomatoes
2 small red peppers
2 small green peppers
2 small yellow peppers
2 tablespoons tomato purée, mixed in 240ml water

Preheat the oven to 180°C/350°F/gas mark 4.

Heat the olive oil in a pan, add the onions and stir until softened. Add the mince and stir until it changes colour. Add the salt, pepper, Lebanese seven spice mix and pine nuts. Stir until the meat is cooked – this will take about 20 minutes. Remove from the heat and set aside.

Cut the top off the tomatoes and scoop out the insides. Do the same with the peppers. Fill the vegetables with the mince mixture and put their lids on top. Stand them in rows in a deep baking tray.

Pour the tomato purée mixture over the vegetables and season with salt. Cover the dish with kitchen foil and bake in the oven for 45 minutes or until cooked.

Serve with *roz abiad* (white rice) (see recipe on page 138).

'Basha' is an old Turkish word for a distinguished man, so Daoud Basha must have been an important person.

Serves 4

1kg minced lamb
1 medium onion, finely chopped
100g pine nuts
salt and black pepper
vegetable oil, for deep-frying

for the sauce
2 tablespoons olive oil
2 medium onions, sliced
3 tablespoons tomato purée, mixed in 1.2 litres water

Place the meat in a bowl with the onion, pine nuts, salt and pepper and mix well. Mould the mixture into small balls.

Heat the vegetable oil in a deep-fat fryer or deep, heavy-based saucepan, and deep-fry the meatballs until golden. Remove and set aside to drain on kitchen paper.

Now make the sauce. Heat the olive oil in a saucepan, add the sliced onions and stir occasionally until softened. Add the tomato purée mixture with salt and pepper. Bring to the boil, then reduce the heat and cook for 30 minutes. Lower the meatballs into the mixture and cook for a few more minutes until heated through.

Served with *roz abiad* (white rice) (see recipe on page 138).

Use chicken breasts instead of lamb as an alternative.

Serves 4

500g dried butter beans
2 tablespoons vegetable oil
5 garlic cloves, chopped
300g lamb shoulder, cut into chunks
salt and black pepper
2 tablespoons tomato purée
2 tablespoons chopped coriander
juice of 1/2 lemon (optional)

Bring the beans to the boil in a pan of water until half cooked, then drain.

Heat the oil in a pan and cook the garlic until softened. Add the lamb, salt and pepper and fry gently for about 15 minutes until the meat is browned.

Pour in 1 litre of water, then add the tomato purée and coriander and bring to the boil. Add the boiled beans, reduce the heat and cook gently for 30 minutes.

Squeeze over a little lemon juice, if using, and serve with *roz abiad* (white rice) or *roz bil sha'rieh* (rice with vermicelli) (see recipes on pages 138 and 139).

loubia bil lahma
green bean stew

لوبية باللحمة

The best beans to use for this are green beans from Cyprus – they are wider than the usual French beans you find in the supermarket. You can get them from Middle Eastern stores.

Serves 6

100ml olive oil
1 medium onion, chopped
5 garlic cloves, chopped
500g lamb shoulder, cut into large chunks
500g green beans, cut into 5cm lengths
4 medium tomatoes, finely chopped
2 tablespoons tomato purée, mixed in 700ml water
salt and black pepper

Heat the oil in a pan and add the onion and garlic. Fry for a few minutes until softened, then add the lamb and continue to cook until browned.

Stir in the beans and cook for about 5 minutes. Add the tomatoes followed by the tomato purée mixture. Season with salt and pepper and cook over a low heat for 30 minutes to reduce the liquid until it just covers the meat and beans.

Turn the mixture out on to a serving platter. Serve hot with *roz abiad* (white rice) or *roz bil sha'rieh* (rice with vermicelli) (see recipes on pages 138 and 139).

Serves 4

about 20 large cabbage leaves, separated
6 lamb chops
200g pudding rice, rinsed
500g minced lamb
3 garlic cloves, chopped
salt and black pepper
3 tablespoons ghee (clarified butter)
juice of 2 lemons

Boil the cabbage leaves in a pan of water for about 2 minutes. Drain and set aside to cool. Boil the lamb chops in a pan of water for 5–10 minutes. Drain.

Combine the rice in a bowl with the mince, garlic, salt, pepper and ghee. Spread the cooled cabbage leaves on a flat surface and divide the stuffing equally among them. Mould the mixture in a long thin shape, then fold in the sides of the leaf and roll up in a cigar shape. Repeat with the other leaves.

Arrange the chops in one layer in the bottom of a deep saucepan then place the rolled cabbage leaves side by side in a circular fashion on top of the chops. Season with salt, then place a heavy lid on the cabbage rolls and add enough water to cover the plate by a few centimetres. Pour in the lemon juice and bring to the boil. Reduce the heat and cook for $1^{1}/_{2}$ hours. Drain any excess liquid. Turn upside down on to a serving plate and serve hot.

Small Lebanese aubergines are best for this recipe.

Serves 4

12 small aubergines
vegetable oil, for deep-frying
1 tablespoon olive oil
1/2 onion, chopped
200g minced lamb
salt and black pepper
2 tablespoons tomato purée, mixed in 500ml water

Preheat the oven to 180°C/350°F/gas mark 4.

Peel the aubergines in stripes. Make a slit in each one lengthways, about half the depth of the aubergine.

Heat the vegetable oil in a deep-fat fryer or deep, heavy-based saucepan. Deep-fry the aubergines for about 5 minutes until golden (see picture on the right). Set aside.

Heat the olive oil in a pan, add the onion and stir until tender. Add the mince, salt and pepper, and continue to cook until the meat is browned.

Place the aubergines in a deep baking tray and, using a teaspoon, stuff each one with the meat stuffing.

Pour the tomato purée mixture on top of the aubergines, season with salt and bake in the oven for about 15 minutes.

Serve with *roz abiad* (white rice) (see recipe on page 138).

sanieh batata wa lahma bil ka'ak
baked potato with meat and breadcrumbs

Serves 6

2 tablespoons vegetable oil
1 medium onion, finely chopped
200g minced lamb
1 tablespoon pine nuts
salt and black pepper
4–5 large potatoes, boiled and mashed
3 tablespoons butter
100g dried breadcrumbs

Preheat the oven to 180°C/350°F/gas mark 4.

Heat the vegetable oil in a pan, add the onion and cook, stirring, until tender. Add the meat, pine nuts, salt and pepper and cook, stirring, until the meat is browned.

Place the warm mashed potato in a bowl, add 2 tablespoons of butter and some salt and mix well.

Grease a deep baking tray with the remaining tablespoon of butter. Spread half of the mashed potato in the tray. Spread the meat mixture over in one layer, then spread the rest of the mashed potato on top.

Sprinkle the breadcrumbs on top and bake in the oven for 20 minutes or until golden.

Cut into squares and serve hot or cold with salad or sautéed vegetables.

kharouf mahshi
roast leg of lamb

You can use a larger leg of lamb if you have more people to feed – it will just need longer to cook.

Serves 6

1 leg of lamb, roughly 1kg
salt and black pepper
1 tablespoon vegetable oil
1 medium carrot, chopped
1 medium red pepper, chopped
4 garlic cloves, peeled

for the rice
1 tablespoon olive oil
1 tablespoon pine nuts
1 tablespoon finely chopped onion
150g minced lamb
300g American long-grain rice, soaked in warm water for 30 minutes

Preheat the oven to 240°C/475°F/gas mark 9.

Rub the leg of lamb with salt and pepper. Transfer to a deep baking tray and drizzle with the vegetable oil. Arrange the carrot, pepper and whole garlic cloves around the lamb and pour in about 700ml of water. Cover the tray with kitchen foil and roast in the oven for 1 hour.

Reduce the temperature to 180°C/350°F/gas mark 4 and cook for another hour. Check occasionally and top up with water if necessary.

For the rice, heat the olive oil in a pan and fry the pine nuts and onion until the onion is softened. Add the mince and cook for about 15 minutes, stirring. Add the rice, salt and pepper and stir for 2 minutes, then pour in about 500ml of water and bring to the boil. Reduce the heat and cook for a further 15 minutes. Transfer to a serving plate.

Remove the lamb from the oven. Use a slotted spoon to remove the softened vegetables from the pan and place in a food-processor. Add a little water and whizz to a smooth, runny gravy. Pour into a serving jug.

Carve the lamb into slices and arrange on individual plates. Serve alongside the rice and gravy.

Shawarma **is very popular in Lebanon – it is the same kind of idea as the Turkish doner kebabs, but instead of fatty minced meat, slices of shoulder of lamb and spices are used – it is pure meat. This recipe is a good way of getting the same great taste at home. You will need to marinate the meat overnight so it takes on all the flavours of the spices. Mastic is an aromatic resin that is used to give flavour and is available from Mediterranean food stores.**

Serves 4

1 shoulder of lamb
1/2 orange, sliced
1 lemon, sliced
1 onion
6 garlic cloves
1 bay leaf
pinch of cloves
salt
1 teaspoon mastic powder
1 1/2 teaspoons shawarma spices (available from Mediterranean stores)
300ml malt vinegar
2 tablespoons lemon juice

Cut the meat into very thin, long slices.

Whizz the orange, lemon, onion, garlic, bay leaf, cloves, salt, mastic powder and spices in a blender until fine. Place this mixture in a deep dish. Add 700ml of water, the vinegar and lemon juice. Coat the meat slices in the mixture and leave in the fridge to marinate overnight.

Preheat the oven to 180°C/350°F/gas mark 4.

Remove the meat pieces from the marinade and place them in a deep baking tray, discarding the marinade. Cook in the oven for 20 minutes, turning the pieces every now and then.

Serve in pitta bread with *tarator* (tahini sauce) (see recipe on page 140), pickles and tomatoes.

main courses **109**

shawarma dajaj
chicken shawarma

Serve with mixed pickles (see recipes on pages 142 and 143), *toum* **(garlic sauce) (see recipe on page 140) and pitta bread.**

Serves 4

1kg chicken breasts
juice of 3 lemons
4 cardamom pods
salt and white pepper
150ml white malt vinegar

Cut the chicken pieces into long, thin slices. Put them in a deep dish with the lemon juice, cardamom pods, salt, pepper, vinegar and enough water to cover and leave in the fridge overnight to marinate.

Preheat the oven to 180°C/350°F/gas mark 4.

Remove the chicken from the marinade and place on a baking tray. Cook in the oven for 20 minutes, turning from time to time. Serve.

Serves 4

1 whole chicken, cut into large pieces
salt and black pepper
2 tablespoons vegetable oil
500g potatoes, cut into large chunks
juice of 1 lemon
4 garlic cloves, crushed

Preheat the oven to 180°C/350°F/gas mark 4.

Place the chicken pieces in a deep baking tray, sprinkle with salt, pepper and oil and roast in the oven for 15 minutes, turning regularly.

Place the potatoes in with the chicken and pour in 250ml of water. Cover the tray with kitchen foil and cook in the oven for a further 40 minutes.

Add the lemon juice and garlic and return to the oven for a further 5 minutes.

Leave to rest for 5 minutes before serving.

Serves 6

1 chicken (about 1.5kg), cleaned
salt and black pepper
2 tablespoons vegetable oil
2 tablespoons olive oil
2 tablespoons finely chopped onion
100g minced lamb
50g pine nuts
200g American long-grain rice
1 tablespoon flaked almonds, toasted

Preheat the oven to 240°C/475°F/gas mark 9.

Season the chicken with salt and pepper. Place on a baking tray and pour over the vegetable oil and 100ml of water. Cover the tray with kitchen foil and cook in the oven for 30 minutes.

Turn the oven down to 200°C/400°F/gas mark 6 and cook the chicken for a further 30 minutes.

Meanwhile, heat the olive oil in a pan, add the onion and stir until softened. Add the lamb, pine nuts, salt and pepper, and stir until the meat is tender. Add the rice and stir. Pour in 300ml of water and bring to the boil. Reduce the heat and cook for 15 minutes or until the rice is tender. Transfer the rice mixture to a serving platter.

When the chicken is cooked, cut into large pieces and arrange on top of the rice. Sprinkle with the almonds.

Serve with *laban* (yogurt) (see recipe on page 34) and salads.

moulokhia bil dajaj
jew's mallow with chicken

In Lebanon people buy fresh Jew's mallow leaves in the summer and dry it at home in big batches of 10–15 kilos. This lasts for the year. I buy a big batch of fresh Jew's mallow from Lebanon and dry it myself. Jew's mallow is a vegetable that looks very similar to mint but has a very long stem – it grows to about 1.5 metres high. You can use lamb instead of chicken for this dish if you prefer.

Serves 6

250g dried Jew's mallow leaves (*moulokhia* leaves)
1kg whole chicken
2 tablespoons vegetable oil
4 tablespoons ghee (clarified butter)
2 onions, finely chopped
3 garlic cloves, crushed
1 tablespoon ground coriander
1 teaspoon dried red chilli flakes
a handful of chopped coriander
salt
juice of 3 lemons

Soak the Jew's mallow leaves in water overnight. Drain and wash well until the water runs clear.

Place the chicken in a large pan of water and bring to the boil. Cook for 45 minutes to 1 hour, skimming the scum from the surface every now and then. Drain and reserve the cooking water. Tear the chicken into pieces and set aside.

Heat the oil and ghee in a pan, add the onion and fry until softened. Add the garlic, ground coriander, chilli flakes, fresh coriander and salt. Cook gently for about 5 minutes, stirring. Add the Jew's mallow leaves and cook for 15 minutes over a medium heat, stirring occasionally.

Add the chicken pieces, then pour in enough of the reserved chicken stock to cover by a good few centimetres. Bring to the boil, then reduce the heat and cook for about 45 minutes.

Squeeze the lemon juice on top of the *moulokhia* and remove from the heat.

Serve hot with *roz bil sha'rieh* (rice with vermicelli) (see recipe on page 139).

khoudar bil dajaj
spiced rice with chicken and vegetables

Serves 4

2 tablespoons olive oil
1 tablespoon finely chopped onion
1 chicken, about 1kg, cut into large pieces
2 tomatoes, chopped
4 carrots, sliced lengthways about 3mm thick
1/2 teaspoon Lebanese seven spice mix (see page 98)
salt
4 courgettes, sliced lengthways about 3mm thick
400g American long-grain rice

Heat the olive oil in a large pan, add the onion and stir until softened. Add the chicken pieces and stir every now and then until the chicken starts to cook.

Add the tomatoes and cook for 10 minutes, then pour in 600ml of water. Stir in the carrots, spice mix and salt and cook for a further 10 minutes. Add the courgettes and when cooked, use a slotted spoon to remove the carrots and the courgettes from the pan and set aside to cool. Add the rice to the pan, bring to the boil, then reduce the heat and simmer for 30 minutes.

Use the carrot and courgette strips to line a large bowl in alternating strips. Pack the rice in tightly, then turn out on to a serving plate. Serve with *laban* (yogurt) (see recipe on page 34) or salad.

samak makli
crispy fried fish

In Lebanon red mullet are quite small, the length of a man's finger. They need to be small in order to fry them. Small sea bream can also be used.

Serves 4

10–12 small red mullet, gutted and cleaned
salt and black pepper
5 tablespoons plain flour
vegetable oil, for deep-frying
2 Lebanese breads (see recipe on page 136) or use shop-bought pitta breads
juice of 2 lemons

Sprinkle the fish with salt and pepper, then coat well with flour.

Heat the oil in a deep-fat fryer or deep, heavy-based saucepan. Deep-fry the fish for 10–15 minutes or until golden. Drain and place in a serving dish.

Cut the Lebanese bread into quarters. Fry in the same oil until golden. Drain and serve with the fish. Squeeze over the lemon juice and serve with *moutabal* (smoky aubergine dip) (see recipe on page 36).

You can use other fish if you prefer, such as salmon or sea bass. Use a cooking mat on top of the baking tray if possible – this stops the fish from sticking.

Serves 6

1.5kg whole red snapper, gutted and cleaned
salt
cumin
handful of coriander, finely chopped, plus extra for garnish
6 garlic cloves, crushed
2 medium carrots, grated
1 tablespoon finely chopped green chilli
1 tablespoon olive oil

Preheat the oven to 180°C/350°F/gas mark 4.

Cut slits into the fish, then rub the fish inside and out with salt and cumin.

Combine the coriander, garlic, carrot and green chilli in a bowl. Stuff this mixture into the cavity of the fish, then rub the fish with olive oil.

Place the fish on a baking tray. Cover with kitchen foil and bake in the oven for 1 hour or until the fish is golden brown on both sides.

Serve hot with *tarator* (tahini sauce) (see recipe on page 140) and coriander to garnish.

sayadieh samak
fish with rice

This is good with *tarator* (tahini sauce) (see recipe on page 140) and salad.

Serves 4

1kg whole white fish, such as cod, sea bass, halibut, filleted (bones reserved)
2 tablespoons olive oil
1^{1}/$_{2}$ onions, sliced
50g pine nuts
salt and black pepper
6 cloves
250g American long-grain rice
vegetable oil, for deep-frying

Place the fish bones in a pan with 500ml of water and bring to the boil.
Simmer for 30 minutes to make a stock.

Cut the fish fillets into large chunks. Heat the olive oil in a pan, add a third
of the onions and fry until golden, then add the pine nuts to gently toast
them. Add the fish and stir for 10 minutes. Add the stock, salt, pepper and
cloves, then bring to the boil. Reduce the heat and simmer for about
10 minutes.

Add the rice and bring to the boil again. Reduce the heat and cook for
20 minutes.

Meanwhile, heat the oil in a deep-fat fryer or deep, heavy-based saucepan.
Deep-fry the remaining onions until browned and crisp. Drain.

Transfer the fish and rice on to a serving dish and scatter the browned onions
on top. Serve.

This is a common sight in Beirut. For some people fishing is a hobby, while others make a living out of it. My brother used to fish like these people, spending all his day standing on the rocky seashore. Fishing is a hobby that needs a lot of patience because sometimes you spend hours and hours without catching even a small fish. People often stand there all day long and come home with nothing, but if they do catch something it might be a rabbit fish (a small fish with a nasty spike on the back of its head), black sea bream or wrasse.

Another method people use is nets or cages that they put at the bottom of the sea. Different fish like different bait. You can use dough with a bit of sugar or prawns – red mullet can be caught this way.

sardin makli
fried whitebait

This dish is eaten with toasted bread and *tarator* (tahini sauce) or *moutabal* (smoky aubergine dip) (see recipes on pages 140 and 36).

Serves 4

500g whitebait, gutted and cleaned
salt and black pepper
4 tablespoons plain flour
vegetable oil, for deep-frying
juice of 2 lemons

Rub the fish with salt and pepper, then coat well in flour.

Heat the oil in a deep-fat fryer or deep, heavy-based saucepan. Deep-fry the whitebait for about 15 minutes or until golden and crisp. Drain, squeeze over the lemon juice and serve.

kraidsieh makli
fried jumbo prawns with garlic and coriander

Serves 4

500g fresh jumbo prawns, or frozen, thawed (about 12 prawns)
100g plain flour
salt and black pepper
125ml vegetable oil
1 tablespoon lemon juice
5 garlic cloves, crushed
2 tablespoons chopped coriander

Peel the prawns, remove the black vein that runs along the back, then wash well. Place the flour in a bowl with salt and pepper. Add the prawns, coating them in the flour.

Heat the vegetable oil in a frying pan and fry the prawns, stirring occasionally, until cooked through – this will take about 10 minutes. Drain the prawns and toss with the lemon juice, garlic and coriander. Season with salt and pepper and serve.

This dish is my own invention. It's a good idea to soak the rice in warm water for 30 minutes before starting. This softens it and reduces its cooking time.

Serves 4

1.5kg fresh tiger prawns, or frozen, thawed
5 tablespoons olive oil
$1/2$ small onion, finely chopped
$1/2$ red pepper, finely chopped
$1/2$ green pepper, finely chopped
$1/2$ yellow pepper, finely chopped
300g basmati rice
salt and black pepper
large pinch of saffron

Preheat the oven to 180°C/350°F/gas mark 4.

Peel one third of the prawns, remove the black vein that runs along the back, then wash well. Cut into large chunks.

Heat 4 tablespoons of the olive oil in a deep pan and fry the onion over a low heat for a few minutes. Add the chopped prawns and fry, stirring occasionally, until half cooked. Add the peppers and cook until softened. Cover the pan when not stirring.

Add the rice, stir for a few minutes, then add 600ml of water, salt, pepper and half the saffron. Cover with a lid, bring to the boil and simmer over a low heat for about 15 minutes.

Meanwhile, butterfly the remaining prawns; leave the shells on, slice lengthways but keep them joined at the tail end. Wash thoroughly. Place on a baking tray, drizzle with 1 tablespoon of olive oil and sprinkle with salt, pepper and the remaining saffron. Bake in the oven for 15 minutes.

Serve the rice topped with the butterflied prawns.

shish taouk
grilled chicken

شيش طاووق

See kebabs on the left in the picture opposite.

Serves 4

1kg chicken breast
1 tablespoon olive oil
1 tablespoon tomato purée
1 tablespoon crushed garlic
1 tablespoon garlic sauce (see recipe on page 140), plus extra for dipping
salt and black pepper
juice of 2 lemons

Cut the chicken breasts into 2cm pieces and place in a bowl. Add the olive oil, tomato purée, garlic, garlic sauce, salt, pepper and lemon juice. Mix well to coat the chicken and leave to marinate in the fridge for at least 1 hour or overnight.

Thread the chicken pieces on to skewers and grill for about 10 minutes on the barbecue or under a preheated grill, turning from time to time.

Serve with *toum* (garlic sauce) for dipping and a salad.

farrouge meshwi
barbecued poussin

فروج مشوي

Serves 2

2 poussins
salt and black pepper

Bone the poussins (your butcher can do this for you). Rub with salt and pepper. Grill over charcoal for about 10–15 minutes, turning occasionally.

Cut the poussins into quarters, then serve with *roz abiad* (white rice) and drizzle over *salsa harra* (hot sauce) (see recipes on page 138 and 141).

كفتة مشوية

kofta meshwi
grilled minced lamb on skewers

See kebabs on the right in the picture on page 128.

Serves 4

500g minced lamb
1 medium onion, finely chopped
1 red pepper, finely chopped
a small handful of flat parsley, finely chopped
salt and black pepper

Place the meat in a bowl with the onion, red pepper, parsley, salt and pepper. Mix well, then mould the mixture on to skewers and flatten a little with your fingers. Grill over charcoal for about 10 minutes, turning occasionally, and serve hot with salads.

لحم مشوي

lahma meshwi
grilled lamb on skewers

See middle kebabs in the picture on page 128. Serve this with a simple salad of very finely sliced onion, chopped parsley and sumac. Tomatoes and onions can also be grilled at the same time to add flavour to the meat.

Serves 4

500g best end lamb, cut into chunks
1 teaspoon tomato purée
1 tablespoon olive oil
salt and black pepper

Place the chunks of meat in a bowl and mix with the tomato purée, olive oil, salt and pepper. Refrigerate until needed.

Thread the meat on to skewers and grill for 10–15 minutes over charcoal or under a preheated grill, turning from time to time. Serve immediately.

This guy looks like my grandfather! He had a shop like this in the meat market in Beirut a long time ago. I come from a family of butchers – including my uncles, grandfather and great grandfather on my father's side. My father, despite going into a different business, is very knowledgeable about meat.

Butchers in the meat market sell kebabs from barbecues set up outside their stalls. They have tables and chairs set out so you can sit and eat your kebab with pitta bread. In Lebanon, everyone has a charcoal barbecue at home, usually on their balcony. I have a charcoal grill at home in London, a smaller version of the one I have in the restaurant – it was made for me by a friend. I use it in the garden in the summer. You can cook these recipes under a hot grill at home but the taste just isn't the same and it certainly isn't authentic.

When I go to Lebanon I like to visit the meat market in a city called Nabatiyeh in the south. My grandfather's cousins have a shop there and now it is the younger generation who work there. Their barbecue meat is always fresh and tasty because it is bought from local farms. My family's place is nice and simple and I like to go there because it reminds me of when I was young at my grandfather's place in Beirut.

kraidis meshwi
grilled prawns

Serves 3

6 jumbo prawns
salt and black pepper
juice of 1/2 lemon
1 teaspoon olive oil
3 garlic cloves, crushed

Butterfly the prawns; leave the shells on, slice lengthways but keep them joined at the tail end. Wash thoroughly. Sprinkle the prawns with salt and pepper, then place in a fish iron and grill over charcoal for about 10 minutes, turning from time to time so they cook evenly. Place in a serving dish.

Mix together the lemon juice, olive oil and crushed garlic to make a dressing. Pour over the prawns and serve.

samak meshwi
grilled fish

In Lebanon we use black sea bream, but you can use any small white fish.

Serves 4

2 medium-sized fish, such as sea bass and Dover sole, scaled and washed
salt and black pepper
pinch of ground cumin
2 tablespoons lemon juice
1 teaspoon olive oil
2 garlic cloves, crushed

Mix the salt, pepper and cumin together and rub over the fish and inside the cavity. Place the fish over charcoal and cook for 20 minutes, turning from time to time.

Mix together the lemon juice, olive oil and garlic and pour over the cooked fish. Serve with *salatah lebnanieh* (Lebanese salad) (see recipe on page 31).

ajeen al khobez
bread dough

This dough can be used to make *khobez*, the traditional Lebanese bread shown in the picture on the right, and can also be used to make the breads on pages 69–71.

Makes about 15–20 breads

500g plain flour, plus extra for dusting
1 tablespoon sugar
1 teaspoon salt
1 tablespoon fresh yeast

Put the flour, sugar, salt, yeast and 240ml of water in a large bowl. Mix together, then knead on a lightly floured board until you have a soft dough. Remove and divide into small balls about 6cm wide. Place the balls on a wooden board. Cover with a moistened tea-towel and leave for 15 minutes at room temperature to rise until they double in size.

Dust the balls with flour on both sides and flatten with a rolling pin to form a circle about 2mm in thickness. Place the circles back on the wooden board, cover with a moistened tea-towel and leave to prove for about 30 minutes or until about 1cm thick.

They are now ready to use for the dough recipes on pages 69–71. Alternatively, if using the dough to make Lebanese bread, place on a baking tray and bake in an oven preheated to 200°C/400°F/gas mark 6 for about 5 minutes until golden and puffed up.

عجينة السنبوسك والفطاير

ajeen sambousak
pastry dough

Use this dough for *fatayer bil sabanikh* (spinach pastries), *sambousak jibneh* (cheese pastries) and *sambousak lahma* (meat pastries) (see recipes on pages 67, 66 and 65). It's good to make a big batch of the dough – anything you don't use can be saved and frozen. The pastries themselves keep well in the freezer so, again, freeze a big batch and have them ready for surprise visitors.

Makes enough for two batches of pastries

1kg plain flour
1 teaspoon salt
1 teaspoon sugar
250ml vegetable oil

Place the flour into a dough mixer or food-processor fitted with a dough hook. Make a well in the centre. Add the salt, sugar and oil and process to a smooth mixture – it will take about 15 minutes. Gradually pour in about 500ml of tepid water, continuing to process in the mixer, until you have a dough the same consistency as bread dough.

Remove the dough and knead for a few seconds with your hands. Cut into two pieces and wrap in clingfilm. Leave to rest at room temperature for about 1 hour before using.

رز أبيض

roz abiad
white rice

Serves 4

250g American long-grain white rice
salt
1 tablespoon vegetable oil

Put the rice in a bowl, cover with warm water and leave to soak for about 30 minutes.

Fill a saucepan with water, add the salt and oil and bring to the boil. Drain the rice and add to the boiling water. Bring back to the boil, then reduce the heat and cook for 10 minutes. Drain the rice of any excess water. Transfer to a serving dish and serve.

Serve with meat courses and barbecue dishes.

Serves 4

1 tablespoon olive oil
100g frozen peas
1 tablespoon finely chopped red pepper
1 tablespoon finely chopped green pepper
250g American long-grain white rice, soaked in warm water for 15 minutes
salt and black pepper

Heat the oil in a saucepan and add the peas and peppers. Cook for about
5 minutes, stirring.

Add the rice to the pan along with salt and pepper and stir well. Pour in
400ml of water and bring to the boil. Cover the pan, reduce the heat and
cook for a further 15 minutes until the rice is tender and has absorbed all
the water. Serve.

**Serve with any main dishes with sauce, such as *moulokhia bil dajaj* (Jew's
mallow with chicken), *bamia bil lahma* (okra with meat), *fasoulieh bil lahma*
(butter bean stew) and *loubia bil lahma* (green bean stew) (see recipes on
pages 114, 97, 101 and 102).**

Serves 4

1 tablespoon olive oil
50g vermicelli, crushed by hand
250g American long-grain rice
salt

Heat the oil in a medium frying pan, add the vermicelli and fry until
browned.

Pour in 400ml of water and stir well. Add the rice and salt. Bring to the boil,
then cover the pan, reduce the heat and cook for 15 minutes until the rice is
tender and has absorbed all the liquid. Serve.

توم
toum
garlic sauce

This recipe makes quite a large quantity, but it will keep in the fridge for a week. It's used as the base of the marinade for *shish taouk* (grilled chicken) (see recipe on page 129) and the sauce for *sawda dajaj* (fried chicken livers) (see recipe on page 76). If you have any left over, it is also good with chips!

Serves 8 (makes enough to be used as a marinade in two recipes in this book)

2 garlic heads, cloves peeled
1 teaspoon salt
1 egg white
500ml vegetable oil
juice of 2 lemons, or more to taste

Put the garlic cloves and salt in a blender or food-processor and whizz to a smooth purée. Add the egg white and whizz again until smooth. With the motor running, very slowly pour in the vegetable oil in a constant, steady stream until all the oil is used up and the sauce is the consistency and colour of mayonnaise. Add the lemon juice and keep whizzing until smooth. Taste and add more if necessary. Serve.

طراطور
taratour
tahini sauce

This is used for the *kofta bil tahina* (kofta with tahini) and served on the side with *falafel* (broad bean patties), *sayadieh* (fish with rice) and *kofta meshwi* (grilled minced lamb on skewers) (see recipes on pages 84, 74, 130 and 120).

Makes about 200ml

200ml tahini
salt
juice of 1 lemon

Place the tahini in a bowl. Add salt to taste, then gradually pour in about 400ml of water, whisking, until it is the consistency of a sauce.

Whisk in the lemon juice and serve.

Serve with grilled chicken or lamb dishes.

Serves 8

1 tablespoon olive oil
1 tablespoon finely chopped onion
1 teaspoon crushed garlic
1 tablespoon finely chopped red pepper
3 tablespoons finely chopped green chillies
1 x 440g tin of plum tomatoes
salt and black pepper

Heat the olive oil in a pan. Add the onion, garlic, red pepper and chilli and cook, stirring, for 10 minutes.

Add the plum tomatoes, salt and pepper. Mix well, breaking up the tomatoes. Bring to the boil, then reduce the heat and simmer for a further 20 minutes. Serve hot.

كبيس القرنبيط

kabis karnabeet
pickled cauliflower

When I make pickles I usually do five or six jars at a time as they last for a long time. You need to store different kinds of pickles in different jars. Beetroot is used to turn the vegetables pink.

Makes 2 litres

1 large head of cauliflower, cut into small florets
250ml malt vinegar
2 tablespoons coarse salt
1 small beetroot, sliced (optional)

Place the cauliflower florets in a 2-litre jar with an airtight lid.

Mix together the vinegar, salt and 1 litre of water. Pour into the jar and add the beetroot, if using. Close the jar tightly. The pickles will be ready to serve in 3–4 weeks.

كبيس الملفوف

kabis malfouf
pickled cabbage

Makes 2 litres

1 white cabbage
250ml malt vinegar
2 tablespoons coarse salt
1 beetroot, sliced

Separate the cabbage into leaves and place them in a 2-litre jar with an airtight lid.

Mix together the vinegar, salt and 1 litre of water and pour into the jar. Add the beetroot and close the lid tightly. Leave for 3–4 weeks, after which it will be ready to use.

The small French turnips are best to use. Don't use the big ones with tough skin – they don't work so well.

Makes 2 litres

10–15 small turnips
250ml malt vinegar
2 tablespoons coarse salt
1 beetroot, sliced

Cut the turnips into fat batons, the size of chunky chips. Place the turnip pieces in a 2-litre jar with an airtight lid.

Mix together the vinegar, salt and 1 litre of water and pour into the jar. Add the beetroot and close the lid tightly. Leave for 3–4 weeks before using.

Makes 2 litres

10–15 small finger-sized cucumbers
250ml malt vinegar
2 tablespoons coarse salt

Place the cucumbers in a 2-litre jar with an airtight lid.

Mix together the vinegar, salt and 1 litre of water and pour into the jar. Close the lid tightly and leave at room temperature for 3–4 weeks before using.

ashtalieh قشطلية
cream pudding

I use a brand called *Puck* for the cream cheese. It comes in 170g tins and can sometimes be found in Middle Eastern stores. Otherwise any cream cheese will do. *Ashtalieh* will keep in the fridge for a couple of days.

Serves 6

1 litre milk
2 tablespoons sugar
5 tablespoons cornflour
2 tablepoons plain flour
2 x 170g tins of cream cheese spread
1 x 10g packet mastic powder
1 teaspoon orange blossom water
1 teaspoon rose water

to finish
50g pine nuts, soaked overnight in cold water
50g peeled almonds, soaked overnight in cold water
50g unsalted pistachios
kater (sugar syrup) (see recipe on page 149)

Heat the milk, sugar, cornflour, flour and half the cream cheese in a pan over a medium heat, stirring all the time with a balloon whisk until the sugar dissolves. Bring to the boil, then reduce the heat and continue to stir until it thickens.

Add the mastic powder, orange blossom water and rose water and stir for another 5 minutes.

Remove the pan from the heat. Pour the mixture into a shallow serving dish and set aside to cool. Spread the remaining cream cheese on top and store in the fridge until needed.

When ready to serve, divide into pieces, decorate with the nuts and pour over the sugar syrup.

The nuts are soaked overnight in water to make them softer and give them a more subtle flavour. Finish with *kater* (sugar syrup) (see recipe below) if you like.

Serves 6

600ml full-fat milk
2 tablespoons cornflour
3 tablespoons granulated white sugar
1 tablespoon orange blossom water
1 tablespoon rose water
100g mixture of pine nuts, unblanched almonds and pistachio nuts,
  soaked overnight in water

Place the milk in a saucepan with the cornflour and sugar. Bring to the boil, stirring all the time with a balloon whisk. Reduce the heat and keep whisking for 10 minutes. Remove from the heat and stir in the orange blossom water and rose water.

Pour into serving dishes and leave to cool. Chill until ready to serve.

Drain the nuts and peel the almonds and pistachios, discarding the skins. Chop very finely, then sprinkle over the top of the puddings and serve.

Use in *ashtalieh* (cream pudding) (see recipe on page 146) or *mouhallabia* (milk pudding) (see recipe above).

250g granulated white sugar
1 teaspoon lemon juice
1 teaspoon rose water
1 teaspoon orange blossom water

Heat the sugar and 125ml of water in a pan over a medium heat until the sugar has dissolved.

Add the lemon juice and bring to the boil. Simmer for 2 minutes, then stir in the rose water and orange blossom water. Leave to cool.

custard with biscuits
custar ma bescout

Serves 8

1 litre full-fat milk
6 tablespoons custard powder
7 tablespoons sugar
3–4 tablespoons cocoa powder
15 digestive biscuits, crushed

Place the milk, custard powder and 6 tablespoons of sugar in a large saucepan over a medium heat and bring to the boil, stirring all the time with a balloon whisk. Reduce the heat and cook for 15 minutes, whisking all the time until thickened.

Meanwhile, mix together the cocoa powder, remaining sugar and 1 tablespoon of warm water to make a paste.

Spread the crushed biscuits in a high-sided dish measuring 30cm x 20cm. Pour the custard over the biscuits, then spread the cocoa paste over the top using a spatula. Refrigerate for 1 hour before serving.

bae'lewa

Bae'lewa or 'baklava' are sweets made from many layers of filo pastry, filled with nuts, such as almonds, pistachios, cashews, and brushed with sugar syrup.

I haven't included a *bae'lewa* recipe because it is very complicated to make at home and you can easily buy good, inexpensive *bae'lewa*. The recipes in this chapter are the kind of desserts you would eat at home in Lebanon, whereas *bae'lewa* is saved for special occasions.

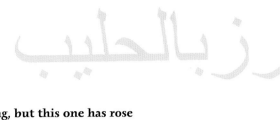

رز بالحليب

riz bil halib
rice pudding

**Not so different to the western-style rice pudding, but this one has rose
water and orange blossom water for flavour and is finished with pistachios.**

Serves 6–8

250g pudding rice
1 litre milk
400g caster sugar
1 tablespoon rose water
1 tablespoon orange blossom water
5 tablespoons pistachios, soaked overnight in water and peeled, to serve

Put the rice and 600ml of water in a pan and bring to the boil. Reduce the
heat and cook for 10 minutes until the rice is half cooked. Drain the rice.

Put the milk and sugar in a separate saucepan and bring to the boil, stirring
all the time with a balloon whisk. Reduce the heat and simmer for 10 minutes,
stirring constantly.

Add the rice and cook for a further 20 minutes, stirring all the time. Remove
from the heat and stir in the rose water and orange blossom water.

Pour into serving glasses and leave until cold. Scatter with the pistachios
and serve.

Moghli is traditionally presented to women after giving birth. A tray of individual puddings are handed round and the new mother chooses first!

Serves 8

300g ground rice
500g caster sugar
1¹/₂ tablespoons ground cinnamon
3 tablespoons ground caraway

to garnish
50g pine nuts, soaked overnight in water
50g almonds, soaked overnight in water
50g pistachios, soaked overnight in water
50g desiccated coconut

Place the ground rice, sugar, spices and 1.5 litres of water
in a pan. Mix well and bring to the boil. Reduce the heat and cook for about
15–20 minutes or until thickened, stirring all the time.

Pour into serving bowls and allow to cool.

Meanwhile, drain the nuts and peel the almonds and pistachios.

Garnish the puddings with the pine nuts, almonds, pistachios and coconut
and serve.

shai bil na'na
mint tea

Mint tea is good to drink at the end of a meal. In Lebanon we drink black tea for breakfast and mint tea after lunch or dinner.

several mint sprigs
sugar (optional)

Bring a pan of water to the boil and add the mint. Simmer for about 10 minutes, then pour into a tea pot. Pour into tea glasses to serve. Add sugar if you wish.

laban ayran
yogurt drink

This goes well with a meal, particularly dishes such as char-grilled meat. You can add a little dried mint if you like but I prefer it without.

Serves 4

450g yogurt (see recipe on page 34) or use shop-bought plain yogurt
pinch of salt (optional)

Put the yogurt and salt in a bowl and whisk in 500ml of cold water to a runny consistency. Set aside in the fridge for at least 1 hour to chill before serving.

You can buy packets of vacuum-packed Lebanese coffee in Middle Eastern shops. It is available with or without cardamom added, as you prefer. We use a *rakweh* to brew the coffee – it looks like a mini saucepan with a long handle. If you haven't got one, use a small saucepan instead. This coffee should be served without milk, like an espresso.

Serves 2

**2 heaped teaspoons ground coffee
a few cardamom seeds, ground (if not already added to the coffee)
sugar, to taste (optional)**

Put all the ingredients in a rakweh or small saucepan with 100ml of water. Place over a medium heat and stir as you bring the mixture to the boil. Simmer for 5 minutes, stirring all the time.

Pour into two cups and serve. The coffee grounds will sink to the bottom of the cups.

This coffee is made of the same mixture as the above recipe but there should be no sugar and more cardamom – the whole cardamom pod is used. The coffee is brewed in a large saucepan over a charcoal fire for three days, until the coffee grounds disappear. This makes it very intense and strong.

Kahwa arabieh is presented on special occasions such as wedding parties and funerals. When it is ready it is poured into decorative coffee pots, which are then offered round with a tray of small cups for the guests. You take a cup of coffee and drink it and you are then offered a second. If you want one you hold your cup out, but if you don't want any more you should shake your cup.

People also go out and sell coffee in the streets from the coffee pots like you see in the picture. Charcoal is put in the top of the pot, which burns to keep the coffee hot.

Weight (solids)

7g	$^1/_4$oz
10g	$^1/_2$oz
20g	$^3/_4$oz
25g	1oz
40g	1$^1/_2$oz
50g	2oz
60g	2$^1/_2$oz
75g	3oz
100g	3$^1/_2$oz
110g	4oz ($^1/_4$lb)
125g	4$^1/_2$oz
150g	5$^1/_2$oz
175g	6oz
200g	7oz
225g	8oz ($^1/_2$lb)
250g	9oz
275g	10oz
300g	10$^1/_2$oz
310g	11oz
325g	11$^1/_2$oz
350g	12oz ($^3/_4$lb)
375g	13oz
400g	14oz
425g	15oz
450g	1lb
500g ($^1/_2$kg)	18oz
600g	1$^1/_4$lb
700g	1$^1/_2$lb
750g	1lb 10oz
900g	2lb
1kg	2$^1/_4$lb
1.1kg	2$^1/_2$lb
1.2kg	2lb 12oz
1.3kg	3lb
1.5kg	3lb 5oz
1.6kg	3$^1/_2$lb
1.8kg	4lb
2kg	4lb 8oz
2.25kg	5lb
2.5kg	5lb 8oz
3kg	6lb 8oz

Volume (liquids)

5ml	1 teaspoon
10ml	1 dessertspoon
15ml	1 tablespoon or $^1/_2$fl oz
30ml	1fl oz
40ml	1$^1/_2$fl oz
50ml	2fl oz
60ml	2$^1/_2$fl oz
75ml	3fl oz
100ml	3$^1/_2$fl oz
125ml	4fl oz
150ml	5fl oz ($^1/_4$ pint)
160ml	5$^1/_2$fl oz
175ml	6fl oz
200ml	7fl oz
225ml	8fl oz
250ml (0.25 litre)	9fl oz
300ml	10fl oz ($^1/_2$ pint)
325ml	11fl oz
350ml	12fl oz
370ml	13fl oz
400ml	14fl oz
425ml	15fl oz ($^3/_4$ pint)
450ml	16fl oz
500ml (0.5 litre)	18fl oz
550ml	19fl oz
600ml	20fl oz (1 pint)
700ml	1$^1/_4$ pints
850ml	1$^1/_2$ pints
1 litre	1$^3/_4$ pints
1.2 litres	2 pints
1.5 litres	2$^1/_2$ pints
1.8 litres	3 pints
2 litres	3$^1/_2$ pints

Length

5mm	$^1/_4$ in
1cm	$^1/_2$ in
2cm	$^3/_4$ in
2.5cm	1in
3cm	1$^1/_4$ in
4cm	1$^1/_2$ in
5cm	2in
7.5cm	3in
10cm	4in
15cm	6in
18cm	7in
20cm	8in
24cm	10in
28cm	11in
30cm	12in

Hussien Dekmak was born in Beirut and has been cooking since he was a teenager. He trained at Al Hamra in London's West End, and opened Le Mignon in 1997 – 'an outpost of classic Lebanese cooking in Camden' (*Time Out*). Hussien sources many of his ingredients such as chick peas, spices and lentils from Lebanon and goes back every summer. This is his first book.

Picture credits

All photography by Martin Brigdale except the following:

Page 15 Bethune Carmichael / Lonely Planet
Page 25 Edward Parker / Alamy
Page 44 World Religions Photo Library,
   www.middleeastpictures.com / Christine Osborne
Page 45 (top) Robert Harding Picture Library Ltd / Alamy
Page 45 (bottom) Ali Kabas / Alamy
Page 72 (top) John Wreford / Alamy
Page 72 (bottom) Robert Harding Picture Library Ltd / Alamy
Page 73 World Religions Photo Library,
   www.middleeastpictures.com / L. Mitchell
Page 92 Char Abumansoor / Alamy
Page 121 John Wreford / Arabian Eye
Page 131 Helene Rogers / Alamy
Page 150 World Religions Photo Library,
   www.middleeastpictures.com / Christine Osborne
Page 155 Roger Wood / CORBIS

Acknowledgements

Thanks go to:

• Kyle Cathie for giving me the chance to introduce this book
• Jenny Wheatley, my editor, for all her help and support
• Martin Brigdale for taking the beautiful photographs
• Helen Trent for all the art that made my cooking look great
• The team at Kyle Cathie Ltd for all their hard work
• My brother Samir for his support and confidence
• Mr Samir Balaghi for his advice
• The many chefs at Al Hamra restaurant I have worked with for teaching me a lot about food
• Zaid Hamandi for supplying all the ingredients for my recipes
• All my friends for supporting me
• All the clients who have eaten my food
• My mother and father for their continuous love and support
• My youngest brother Oussama for his help and all our good work at Le Mignon
• My sister Naife for her help
• My wife Benan for all her love and support